HOW REAL ESTATE CAN BUILD GENERATIONAL WEALTH

PETER SAVIO

TABLE OF CONTENTS

WHY I WROTE THIS BOOK

If you were to ask me why I wrote this book, I would say I wanted to make a difference. My whole real estate career was about helping people. Who am I?

My name is Peter Savio. I was born and raised in Hawaii. I purchased my first property with money from my paper route and odd jobs when I was 15 years old. I teamed up with my older sister, since she was of legal age and could own real estate. All my brothers and sisters (there were five children in the family) purchased real estate as teenagers.

We learned about real estate by listening to our mother explain it to clients who would call her at home with questions. Real estate has always fascinated me. I started helping my mother with her real estate by keeping track of all the listings and sales. (As a fun aside, she was also the agent who worked with the "Rich Dad" referenced in Robert Kiyosaki's book *Rich Dad Poor Dad*.)

Anyhow, I became a real estate junkie, fascinated by everything involving it. I majored in real estate at the University of Hawaii, got my license at 20, and then went into selling for my mother's firm, Tropic Shores Realty Ltd.

After working every day for over a year, however, I decided I was not a good salesperson and opted to give up and quit real estate. I would go back to college and become a history teacher. My mother agreed that I was a horrible salesperson but also asserted that I wasn't the problem. She explained that I did not like the idea of being a salesperson. I saw a salesperson as someone trying to convince another person to do something they really didn't want to do—in this case, to buy real estate.

My mother encouraged me to instead think of a salesperson as a teacher who is educating someone by giving them the information they need to buy. I felt much more comfortable with the idea of teaching my clients about real estate.

As a result, I naturally changed my attitude and approach, and went on to become salesman of the year.

A few years later, I started my own real estate company. It was 1980. I concentrated on helping first-time home buyers enter the market.

No sooner did I start my company, however, than America began going through a very high-interest rate crisis, and mortgage rates were anywhere from 10% to 20%.

Basically, it was killing Hawaii's (and the nation's) housing market.

Under this pressure, I came up with the approach of buying buildings at low prices due to the high interest rates.

Apartment buildings are sold based on income after all expenses, including mortgage payments. At that time, high interest rates wiped out owners' cash flows. For a new buyer, every owner that had to sell needed to reduce their prices. In some cases, if selling was critical, they sold at losses. In short, the prices had to come down so that new owners could make money paying an 18% interest rate.

So, I ended up seeing an opportunity to buy based on high interest rate at a lower price, converting them to condominium apartments and selling them at a cost to first-time buyers. Essentially, I was only making sales commissions for acting as a developer. If a house was appraised at $200,000 but only cost me $90,000, I would sell it for $90,000.

It was basically a cost-plus program sold at cost with a small profit. I've been doing this for over 40 years now, and in the process, have given away approximately $300 million in developers' profit to my 6,000+ buyers in the form of lower prices.

My whole real estate career has not been about money or profit, but rather about helping people and making a difference. My first book was titled *Hawaii's Housing Solution, "Move to the Mainland": 60 Years of Failure, IT MUST END*. It is a book that identified the reason housing was unaffordable and offered a set of solutions to create and keep housing affordable. While written for Hawaii, if you live in an area where housing is unaffordable for the average buyer, my book may offer some solutions, for Hawaii's housing crisis is not unique to the state. My third upcoming book will explain the solution for Hawaii's housing crisis and how to reduce our high cost of living.

This book, my second, is written to educate potential buyers and take away the fear of buying, showing how wealth is created in real estate.

I believe most buyers are unaware of what's covered in this book. Yet, this information would give them (and hopefully, you) the confidence to buy and the knowledge of how to make their purchase more successful by using the wealth creators in the real estate equation to magnify and improve their return or increase in value.

This book can be technical (and even a little bit of a workbook), but I think after you've gone through the process, you'll agree that understanding all these concepts makes you a better real estate buyer and investor.

Good luck, and I hope you enjoy the book as well as your journey through purchasing real estate and creating wealth for yourself and your family.

The key to real estate creating wealth is the realization that everyone needs real estate, we need a place to live and raise our family, and real estate creates wealth for the owner.

Let's begin our journey into understanding how to create wealth.

CHAPTER 1

THE COST OF RENTING

In America, wealth is created through the ownership of real estate. Homeownership may cost more than renting, but it is cheaper than renting over time. Homeownership builds wealth for you, your family, and future generations. Renting takes away your wealth and gives it to the property owner.

This book is going to compare renting to owning real estate over a lifetime. You will see how ownership of real estate creates additional opportunities to make even greater wealth over your lifetime.

You will learn how renting takes wealth away from the tenant and gives it to the property owner.

Ownership of real estate is not only about having a place to live and raise a family but also the opportunity to create wealth and a better life for you and your family.

America has always been about owning real estate. Somehow, we seem to have forgotten the role real estate plays in our lives and the creation of wealth in the future. Our schools and colleges do not teach us the importance of real estate ownership.

THE GREATEST GENERATION STARTED IT ALL.

Our generation had forgotten WHY and HOW wealth was created in real estate. Yet, the answer was given to us by the greatest generation. They came back from WWII and were encouraged by our government to go to college under the GI Bill and buy a home using the Veterans Administration (VA) financing.

Large numbers of them went to college and purchased homes once employed. They started the creation of real estate wealth through the ownership of single-family homes. 50 years later, in the late 1980s and 1990s, they started passing away and leaving large estates to their children and grandchildren. We failed to understand the importance of buying a home to create wealth. We saw the wealth they had created as being due to the college education, better jobs, potential for advancement in employment, and a strong economy. We thought our parents and grandparents were Depression-era babies, frugal and good savers. Why is *all of the above* true, but owning a home is what turned out to be the *greatest* creator of wealth for them?

We know there are advantages to ownership of real estate. We knew it made sense to buy, but many of us did not understand WHY or HOW the wealth was created in real estate.

Like their parents, they also purchased homes because that's what successful people did. We never understood how buying a home would be a major contributor to creating success and wealth.

If you understand real estate's wealth creators, you can then create wealth for yourself and your family by owning a home. You need a place to live, so why not own it and put the wealth creators to work for you?

COMPARING RENTING TO OWNING

Our journey will start in 1965.

I would start our adventure in 2020 and go forward 60 years, but using current values, the numbers would grow so large that over 60 years, we would have trouble believing they were accurate.

Going back 60 years to 1965, however, you can see, understand, and verify the historic values as we bring them up to today's values.

If I had told a buyer in 1965 that their $22,000 home would sell from $700,000 to $1,000,000 within 60 years, they would have laughed and thought I was crazy. Yet today, those are reasonable values in Honolulu, where I live. Each community is different, but if you go back 60 years and look at the values, you will say, "Why didn't my family buy back then? Home prices were so reasonable."

THE SAME IS TRUE FOR RENTING.

If I had told a tenant 60 years ago that their rent of $300 per month would grow to $4,500 or more per month in 2020, they would not have believed me.

But again, go back in time and check your community; from 1965 until today, you will find substantial growth in rent.

In 1965, a million dollars was an unimaginable amount of money. Our country's wealthiest were millionaires, not billionaires. The average person could not imagine being a millionaire—but today, millionaires are common.

SO, WE START OUR JOURNEY IN THE 1960s.

To give context to my concern, let's look at a home in 1965 that was worth $25,000. That home today is worth $700,000 to $1,000,000—an increase of 28 times for $700,000 and 40 times for $1,000,000. If we assume the same thing will happen over the next 60 years (2020 to 2080), then the $700,000 home today could increase in value 28 times and be worth $19,600,000, or a $1,000,000 home could be worth up to $40,000,000. These are good examples of how values going forward seem *unbelievable*.

If we use today as a starting point, the price in 2080 would have to be, at best, an educated guess. Would you have confidence in that number, or just feel it was a wild guess? You can see how using future numbers and projecting 60 years into the future seems way too large. Yet it is exactly what happened over the last 60 years to our 1960s $25,000 home and its owner.

So, it is better to go back in time since the numbers are more believable and provable. We will use the 60 years from 1965 through 2025 in our examples. The 2025 values should be closer to today's values than the original values in the 1960s. We can understand and accept 2025 values because they can easily be verified.

To make our 1965 values more meaningful, I will add two generations to the example; I will add a son and grandson to our family of buyers.

The grandparents, who purchased at age 30, will go from 1965 to 2025 (60 years), so they will be 90 years old.

The son would have purchased at age 20, owning a home from 1985 until 2055 (70 years).

The grandson would have purchased at age 20, owning from 2005 to 2075 (70 years).

The grandson's ownership results are the closest to what would be expected today since he purchased in 2005 and will own his home until 2075 (age 90).

So just remember, the grandson is closest to what you will expect to see in your situation if you are considering buying a property in today's market.

SO, LET'S START OUR 60-YEAR JOURNEY

The first step of our journey is looking at a home in 1965 and comparing renting to buying. That home could be purchased for $25,000. It would have rented for $300 per month. This seems low today. However, back then, it was just as expensive to rent a home as it is today, and as big a challenge as buying a home in the present day. Nothing has changed except the property's dollar amount.

It is important to remember that rents were lower in 1965, and so were incomes. Back then (like today), rents were supposed to be 30% to 35%

of your income. So, the number is larger today, but the ratio is the same. This ratio was determined to be *what works* in most scenarios when it comes to housing.

Let's also assume the home will be rented in 1965 by a 30-year-old couple, Mr. and Mrs. Tenant. In our example, we will follow them and their family over 60 years and compare renting costs to buying. So, 60 years later in 2025 and at the age of 90, the Tenants are paying rent of $3,000 per month. We will assume the average rent was $1,650 per month over the 60 years they were renting. The rent paid by the Tenants over 60 years is $1,188,000. That is the total rent paid for a home they could have purchased for $25,000.

In reality, the Tenants (who have been renters their entire lives) have nothing to show for it but a stack of rent receipts.

The obligation to pay rent continues as long as the Tenants are living. When they retire at the age of 70, their retirement incomes will remain stable, but their monthly rent will continue to increase. As a result, the Tenants' financial life may become more of a struggle. This is true for many renters. By always renting, they have none of the benefits of the wealth creators in real estate. They have, however, created financial pressure to pay ever-increasing rent.

The Tenants can also expect increases in other living costs, including medical, food, transportation, and clothing. Inflation causes prices to increase over time, adding even more pressure on the Tenants to maintain a comfortable lifestyle.

Their retirement years have become a struggle to survive because they are living on a fixed income. They may need their family or government assistance to help them in their final years. That cost, if not paid for by the family, will be paid for by their children's and grandchildren's taxes. There's really no need for this to happen, and it could have been avoided if they had only owned a home during their lifetime rather than renting one.

WHAT WOULD HAVE HAPPENED IF THE TENANTS HAD PURCHASED THE FIRST HOUSE THEY RENTED?

WHAT ASSUMPTIONS ARE WE MAKING?

If the Tenants had purchased the first house they rented in 1965, what would the difference be in the cost of owning vs. renting over the 60 years for Mr. and Mrs. Tenant?

Again, to keep the rent vs. buy examples as consistent as possible, we will assume no down payment on the purchase since no down payment is required to rent. We will assume the rental security deposit is equal to the buyers' closing costs.

Since we assume no money down is required, the Buyers used 100% financing through the Veterans Administration VA loan program. A good interest rate for a mortgage in 1965 would have been 6%. The loan's term (or amortization) would have been 30 years. Also, it would have been a simple interest, fixed-rate loan, which is the most common loan used in America to finance residential real estate. This means the total monthly mortgage payment (which is made up of principal and interest) remains the same for the entire loan term. However, the allocation of the payment to principal and interest changes monthly due to the remaining balance of the loan being reduced by the monthly principal paid. Every month, the balance owed on the mortgage goes down as the principal is credited for that month. Interest is computed on the remaining principal balance owed, so every month, interest goes down, and more funds from payment are available to pay off the remaining loan balance. The loan balance (principal) owed is reduced monthly by the portion of the monthly payment applied to the principal for that month.

WHAT DO THE NUMBERS LOOK LIKE?

In our example, the gross rent in 1960 was about $300 monthly. So again, the same assumptions will be made.

Landlord's application for the $300 rental payment made by Mr. and Mrs. Tenant:

- ❖ $150 Landlord's mortgage (6% on $25,000 mortgage)
- ❖ $50 Insurance and property tax
- ❖ $50 Utilities
- ❖ $50 Landlord's profit

We are using the principal and interest payment on the loan in all our examples.

We will assume our young couple, Mr. and Mrs. Buyer, can pay $150 per month to purchase a home. This means they could buy a three-bedroom home for $25,000 in 1960 in one of Honolulu's newer communities.

TOTAL PRINCIPAL AND INTEREST PAID FOR LOAN TERM

The monthly payment can be made using an amortization schedule or a computer program. You need to know the:

1. Amount to be financed
2. Interest rate on comparative loans
3. Term of the loans (usually 15 to 30 years)

The calculation for determining the total principal and interest paid over 30 years is to multiply the total monthly payment by 360 months. That will give you the total principal and interest paid over 30 years. So, the math looks like this:

MONTHLY PRINCIPAL AND INTEREST PAYMENT

MORTGAGE PAYMENT X MONTHS OF TERM LOAN = TOTAL PRINCIPAL AND INTEREST PAID OVER LOAN TERM

$150 X 360 MONTHS (30 YEARS) = $54,000

Since we're calculating the total of all principal and interest (the mortgage) payments made over the 30-year term, subtract the principal paid. This is the beginning mortgage balance of $25,000. Thus, the math will look like this:

> $54,000 = TOTAL PRINCIPAL AND INTEREST PAID OVER 30 YEARS
>
> ($25,000) = BEGINNING MORTGAGE BALANCE WHICH IS PAID OFF AFTER 30 YEARS
>
> $ 29,000 = INTEREST PAID OVER 30 YEARS

Now, you can see that buying a home costs $29,000 in interest. Interest is an expense that is paid to the bank. Remember, the interest paid is tax deductible and you get a portion back in the form of a tax refund. In our analysis we are using a hypothetical combined 28% federal and state income tax bracket.

The $25,000 paid as principal has created an asset—a debt-free home. Paying off the loan took 30 years, and the home has become an investment in the future. You no longer have a mortgage payment.

So, for the next 30 years, what would have been rent, or mortgage payments would be yours to spend or invest as you wish.

All pay raises during the 30 years of the loan and all future pay raises are yours since you have no mortgage payment or rent to pay going forward. You locked in a constant monthly payment by having a loan, and now that it is paid off, all of that payment is yours.

The cost of renting over 60 years for Mr. and Mrs. Tenant is $1,188,000. The cost to buy for Mr. and Mrs. Buyer was $29,000 in interest expense over 30 years. Remember, there is still a refund on taxes paid, reducing interest expense. For the remaining 30 years, they do not have any mortgage payments. The savings for our Buyers' families due to purchasing their home rather than renting are $1,159,000.

Remember, unlike rent, the mortgage payment did not increase over the 30 years. That made it easier for our family, the Buyers, to enjoy a better life due to home ownership. As we continue our story, we realize it only improves because ownership creates wealth over time.

No question, owning your home is less expensive than renting. Whether buying like the Buyer family or renting like the Tenant family, you create wealth. The question in real estate is, who gets the wealth created? The Buyer family keeps the wealth produced, whereas the Tenant family gives the wealth to their landlord through the rent they pay.

OWNERSHIP COSTS REMAIN THE SAME, BUT RENT CHANGES REGULARLY.

Owning locks in the cost of housing through a mortgage payment that will remain constant. However, if you are renting, you can expect to see increases in annual rent. Even if you get a pay raise, a large portion of that will likely be used to pay rent increases. Renting converts pay raises to higher and higher rent. At the same time, home ownership saves pay raises because monthly mortgage payments remain constant. Pay raises result in extra cash for the Buyer family to spend rather than paying the landlord's higher rent like the Tenant family does. The pay raises, if invested, could generate millions in asset value. Over time, buying is always cheaper than renting.

You can clearly see how renting did not create wealth for the tenants; instead, it took wealth from the family.

The Tenant family of renters created wealth for the landlord. The $1,159,000 would have belonged to the Tenant family if they owned it instead of renting it. As a renter, the potential wealth creators do not go to the tenant who is paying rent. Instead, the wealth went from the tenant to the landlord. Just think about it—if the Tenant's family had just purchased the property for $25,000 instead of renting, that wealth would have gone to their family.

IN SUMMARY

❖ All the property value being created by ownership is passed to the landlord's family since they are the property owner.

❖ The tenants are giving their family's wealth to the landlord's family.

❖ The tenants are giving away their family's opportunity and future to the landlord.

❖ Remember, everyone needs a place to live, and everyone creates wealth in real estate. The question is, are you building wealth for yourself and your family, or for your landlord and his family?

❖ There are a total of 12 wealth creators embedded in the ownership of real estate, nine in residential real estate, and three additional wealth creators in investment real estate. All wealth creators are working to create wealth for the property owner.

❖ That owner should be you and your family.

❖ That wealth created through real estate could mean a better standard of living, vacations, better schools and/or college educations, and money to start a business or invest. The decision is yours whether to buy or rent—to create wealth for yourself or for your landlord.

WHAT WE HAVE LEARNED IN CHAPTER 1

1. Rent is paid to the landlord.

2. Rent pays taxes on the landlord's mortgage and his cost of ownership.

3. Landlords make a profit from renters.

4. Renting creates wealth for the landlord.

5. Rent is paid forever—it never stops.

6. Rent is a tenant giving away his family's opportunity and wealth to the landlord.

7. A mortgage has a constant monthly payment.

   ❖ Mortgage payments benefit owners since they are buying a capital asset.

8. Income increases over time, but a large part goes to the payment of the tenants' rent increases.

   ❖ If you own your home, your monthly payment on a mortgage remains the same, and any pay increases are yours to spend. *(*Hint: the fixed payment is one of the wealth creators.)*

9. A family will save millions of dollars if they buy rather than rent.

   ❖ The wealth created by owning a home (particularly the constant monthly payment) provides you with greater accessibility to the following opportunities because future increases are now available that would have otherwise gone to increased rents. Such as . . . affording a better education for your children, money to start a business, a better retirement. Pay raises can be spent on an improved style of living in lieu of rent increases.

10. Ownership should be a well-thought-out strategy for creating wealth through real estate ownership.

11. Understanding real estate and how it creates wealth makes buying easier because it takes the mystery out of buying.

    ❖ Ownership may start off being more expensive than renting, and it may require a sacrifice for a few years, but it's always cheaper than renting over time.

12. You can accelerate the wealth creators by understanding them.

13. We are starting in 1965 and moving forward through 2025, a period of 60 years.

    ❖ We have gone back in time because the values make more sense.

14. The average rent is $1,650 for the 60-year period we are studying.

15. The total rent paid over 60 years is $1,188,000.

16. Our tenant starts renting at the age of 30 and will be 90 years old in 2020.

17. All our calculations use a lifetime of 90 years.

    ❖ Rent and rent increases must be paid as long as you live. Remember, rent increases over time.

18. When you retire, incomes are reduced, but all expenses continue to rise—especially rent. Housing is usually your biggest monthly expense.

    ❖ If our renter had purchased, the price in 1960 would have been $25,000.

19. If our renter had paid a monthly rent of $300, we would assume $150 was paid to the landlord's mortgage.

20. Our renter could have used that $150 per month to qualify for a $25,000 home using 100% financing.

    ❖ The principal and interest paid over 30 years would be $54,000. If the $25,000 principal is subtracted, the interest paid is $29,000. Interest is tax deductible, so the interest paid of $29,000 is gross paid and the actual is less dependent upon tax bracket.

❖ Renting over 60 years cost $1,188,000. The cost of buying was the interest expense of $29,000. Thus, the savings due to owning the property are $1,159,000. *Note that this is not even inflation-adjusted, so the nominal dollar total is even higher.

21. Whether you buy or rent, you are creating value. The difference is whether the value you create goes to the landlord. The question is, who gets the value—you and your family or the landlord and his family?

22. Value created in real estate goes to the owner of the property.

23. Tenants create value for the owner.

24. Everyone needs a place to live. Creating value in real estate is the bonus given to OWNERS.

25. There is no question that it is best to be the owner.

26. The wealth created could have improved your style of living and been used to start a business or send your children to a better school or college. The wealth created could have been invested, thus creating more wealth.

27. Understanding how value is created in real estate will give you the knowledge and confidence to buy wealth and build a future for you and your family.

CHAPTER 2

THE COST OF RENTING OVER THREE GENERATIONS

Remember how we did the calculation for Mr. and Mrs. Tenant who, at age 30, rented a home for their new family. It was rented for over 60 years starting in 1965 compared to buying that same home. But during that period, the Tenant family had children and grandchildren who grew up and were ready to purchase a home. Let's see what would have happened had the younger Tenants been forced to rent and unable to buy their own homes. Understanding the potential, you create for your family by owning real estate is essential. If you are willing to make sacrifices for a few years, you can start the creation of wealth for yourself and future generations.

If parents rent, there is a good chance their children will also rent. If parents own their home, there is a good chance the children will own their home as well.

Since we are comparing the cost of renting to owning over a long period, we should also compare renting and owning for the children and grandchildren.

The Tenant family has the potential to create additional wealth during the parents' lifetime by helping their children and grandchildren buy a home. So, let's do a quick analysis comparing renting to owning, assuming the parents, the son, and the grandson all purchased a property. This will give us a true picture of what a family can do as a group by helping each other purchase property.

Let's start with the rent vs. buy calculation for the Tenant family. We are taking a snapshot in time in 2025 when the parents are 90, and their son (who was born in 1965) is now 60 years old. The grandson (who was born in 1985) is 40 years old.

The first generation: THE PARENTS are 90 years old in 2025.

Earlier, we did the rent vs. own analysis of the first generation. The rental cost over the 60 years was $1,188,000.

The second generation: THE SON, born in 1965, is now 60 years old.

We will look at the son's position in 2025. The following analysis is for the 60-year-old son who moved out of his parents' home at the age of 20 and rented a home from 1985 until 2020. Over the 40 years of renting, the average rent for his family was $1,500 per month. After 40 years (or 480 months) of paying rent, the son has spent $720,000 up until 2025.

The third generation: THE GRANDSON, born in 1985, is 40 years old in 2025.

The grandson moved out of his parents' home in the year 2005 at 20, becoming the third generation to rent a home. In 2025, at 40, he has been renting for 20 years. His average monthly rent was $2,000. After 20 years, his family has paid $480,000 in rent.

WHAT IS THE TENANT FAMILY'S TOTAL COST OF RENTING IN 2025?

The parents have paid rent totaling $1,188,000 for 60 years.

The son, who is 60 years old, has paid rent totaling $720,000 after renting for 40 years.

The grandson is now 40 and has paid rent totaling $480,000 over 20 years.

You can see that three generations of tenants have paid $2,388,000 in rent but have not created any wealth for themselves because they were renting. They were great renters who always paid their rent on time, but they created no wealth for themselves because they rented.

The rent they paid has improved their landlord's quality of life and wealth, who purchased several investment homes from the profit of the rent paid by our three-generational family, the Tenants. Our family of renters has given away their wealth and potential for a better life to the landlord and his family.

WHAT WE HAVE LEARNED IN CHAPTER 2

1. We analyzed one couple and determined the cost of renting and the cost of owning.

2. It's important to realize that sacrificing to buy a home should start a process of creating value over many generations.

3. In our example, we assume the first generation is the parents. The second generation is their son, and the third generation is their grandchild.

4. We did a rent vs. buy calculation for all three generations.

5. The parents rented for 60 years and paid $1,188,800 in rent.

6. The average rent for the son was $1,500 per month. This totaled $720,000. This is the rent paid after 40 years. He still has 30 more years until the age of 90.

7. The grandson paid rent for 20 years. The grandson paid rent of $480,000 over that period. He still has 50 years of paying rent till he reaches the age of 90.

8. The parents (at age 90), the son (at age 60), and the grandson (at age 40) have paid $2,388,000 in rent.

9. The rent and wealth they created have improved their landlord's quality of life and increased their family's wealth.

CHAPTER 3

THE COST OF RENTING FOR OUR THREE-GENERATION FAMILY

Let's take our three generations of renters and convert them to owners so that we can accurately see the difference between renting and owning over a period of 90 years. If parents are homeowners, there is a good chance their children will also be homeowners. The parents have set a good example for their children, showing that home ownership is attainable.

EQUALIZING THE EXAMPLES

In our earlier example, the parents/grandparents rented and/or owned up to the age of 90. To be accurate in our comparison, we have to equalize the period for renting by using a 90-year lifetime for the son and grandson. This means the son (born in 1960) lives until 2050. His son/original Buyer's grandson (who was born in 1980) will live until 2070. When you are a renter, you must pay rent all your life.

As a homeowner, you pay a mortgage for 30 years, but you are creating wealth throughout your life. We get a true picture of the magnitude of the savings for this family by looking at the savings generated over their lifetimes. We can assume some of this wealth was passed from generation to generation. Still, we do not account for that in this analysis. The additional wealth generated through those savings can be staggering! We are only looking at the potential savings of each of the Buyers' three-generational families.

We also get an idea of how rent increases from one generation to another. Remember, this is only the savings when comparing renting to owning. It does not include the bulk of wealth created through real estate. Those savings will be covered in future chapters.

WHAT IS THE TOTAL COST OF RENTING FOR OUR FAMILY, ASSUMING EACH GENERATION LIVES TO BE 90?

The son paid an average monthly rent of $2,500 over 70 years and will conservatively pay $2,100,000 in rent over his lifetime.

The grandson's average rent for 70 years was $3,500 per month, resulting in a total rent paid over his lifetime of $2,940,000.

The actual rent increases from 2025 until 2055 and 2075 will be much higher than what I am showing. As explained in Chapter 1, I used actual numbers from 1960 until 2020 because the projected numbers were so large. The future numbers will appear so large that they may seem unbelievable. Focus on the concept rather than the dollar amount.

FAMILY'S COST OF RENTING

The family's actual cost of renting for the three generations of Tenants in 2020 was $2,388,000 when they were 90, 60, and 40 years old. The parents paid rent until 90 years old for a total of $1,188,000. If their son had paid rent until he was 90, he would have paid $2,100,000. The grandson paid rent totaling $2,940,000 until he was 90 years old. The total rent paid over the lifetime of three generations is $6,228,000. This is the number we will use to pay for the total rent going forward. Don't forget the numbers in our example, which started in 1965 when rents and prices were much lower.

It is important to look at the values in your area to compare the rents and home values. You can then estimate the future values. Real estate is local, so values represent employment incomes in the market where you live. Realize that your amounts could be larger or smaller than the ones used here, but the concept remains the same. The definition of a real estate market where there is no outside distortion is a market where income determines the sales price of homes. It is the simplest way to determine a local real estate market's local sales price.

Usually, the first distortion is moving from a local to a national market. Basically, that's where other US buyers from outside the community buy property in the community you are looking at. They could be buying for investment, buying to retire, or buying a vacation home. The key is the price they pay. Their purchase price has nothing to do with local wages but everything to do with what that outside buyer can pay.

In Hawaii, the national market started to show distortions in our local market as early as 1960. The early distortion was caused by mainland investor buyers and retirees moving to Hawaii. More pressure on price was added by federal employees and military housing allowances. That was soon followed by increases in Section 8 rents. Section 8 is a federal rental housing subsidy program, but as our market distorted value, rents also began to increase and were no longer tied to wages in the community. To overcome this rental shortage, the State of Hawaii applied for and was granted additional Section 8 funds to pay above-market rents. This was needed so that they could attract units for Section 8 tenants. This is a case of a distortion causing an additional distortion.

The international market is the distortion caused by buyers from around the world purchasing property in Hawaii. Again, in this case, the price has no relationship to local wages or the local market. The international market has no ties to what buyers in the national market could afford to pay. International buyers tend to be wealthier and willing to pay a premium to get the property and the location they want.

Most international cities are recognizable worldwide. I checked the Internet to get a list of international cities, and it was more expensive than I would've thought. It makes perfect sense when you consider the quality of the cities or their location. The list included Paris, Tokyo, New York, Barcelona, Dubai, Hong Kong, Bangkok, Istanbul, Singapore, Rome, Seoul, and of course, we can't forget to add Honolulu.

Attracting international appeal leads to the increase in prices Hawaii is now experiencing due to worldwide appeal.

One must look at their market and compare prices to wages or income. If affordability is an issue, outside buyers are most likely purchasing and can usually pay more than local wages allow.

Also, remember that the original example started with a rent of $300. It went up 10 times over the 60 years in the first example. The asset's value increased 28 times from $25,000 to $700,000. In the example going forward, a smaller increase was used since we are showing the concept, not predicting the future value of rent or the future value of a home. Even though we are being conservative, the numbers are impressive. It is safe to assume that the actual rent and the homes' value would be greater in 2050 and 2070 than the amounts projected. Don't focus on the numbers; understand the concept.

WHAT WE HAVE LEARNED IN CHAPTER 3

1. We continue the comparison of renting vs. owning.

2. Rent is paid forever, rent creates no wealth, and rent is an obligation, while purchasing and ownership are paid for the term of the mortgage loan, and then after that, no payments are made.

3. To make an accurate comparison, we must assume that the Buyer family will all rent and own until the age of 90.

4. Our earlier comparison was a snapshot of what was paid in rent when the parents were 90, the son was 60, and the grandson was 40 years old.

5. Assuming the Buyer family members all live to the age of 90, we get a true picture of the family's savings.

6. Remember, we are only looking at wealth created by purchasing. Additional wealth creators will be covered in later chapters.

7. The savings realized in purchasing rather than renting are large but are only a tiny part of the wealth created by real estate.

8. The son's average rent until 90 is $2,500 per month.

9. The grandson's average monthly rent until 90 is $3,500.

10. The parents' total rent paid is $1,188,000 for 60 years.

11. The son's total rent paid is $2,100,000 for 70 years.

12. The grandson's total rent paid is $2,940,000 for 70 years.

13. The cost of renting for three generations is $6,228,000.

14. If you prepared a rent vs. buy comparison worksheet today, you would start with today's rents and home prices.

15. Wealth is created by purchasing, thus providing a better and more financially comfortable life for you and your family.

16. Sacrifices are required to purchase a home, but the rewards are well worth it.

17. Remember, we are using present rents and increasing them monthly by less than the historic increases from 1965 until 2020.

Our future estimates are very conservative, and actual rents are anticipated to be much higher.

THE COST OF OWNING FOR OUR THREE-GENERATION FAMILY

THE FIRST GENERATION - THE PARENTS

You will remember that the cost to purchase a home in 1965 was $25,000 with a monthly payment of $150 at 6% interest on a 30-year loan. The total principal and interest paid was $54,000, of which the interest expense was $29,000.

Once the loan is paid off after 30 years, the parents own the home debt-free. We know the interest expense (or the cost of buying) was $29,000. Subtracting the interest (the cost of buying a home) from the rent that would have been paid will give us the savings realized by purchasing instead of renting. The interest of $29,000 was subtracted from the total rent paid by the grandparents for a savings of $1,159,000 by purchasing.

THE SECOND GENERATION - THE SON

The son also rented a home from the age of 20. His initial monthly rent was $1,500. This would have qualified him for a mortgage of $350,000. Like his parents, he chose a 30-year fixed-rate loan, so his mortgage payments remained the same; so, the total principal and interest paid was $540,000. The beginning balance of $350,000 is subtracted, leaving $190,000 in interest paid. If $2,100,000 is the total rent paid by the son and purchasing the home costs $190,000 in interest. Compared to renting, the son would have saved $1,910,000 over his lifetime.

THE THIRD GENERATION - THE GRANDSON

The grandson's initial monthly rent was $2,000. This would have qualified him to purchase a $500,000 home for which the total principal and interest paid over 30 years is $720,000. We subtract the principal paid off, $500,000, and the interest paid or cost is $220,000. This is the cost of buying. The grandson's total rent paid was $2,940,000, and the cost to buy it was $220,000, which is a savings in rent of $2,720,000.

THE FAMILY'S TOTAL SAVINGS BY PURCHASING

The first generation saved $1,159,000.

($1,188,000 in rent paid less interest $29,000 = $1,159,000)

The second generation saved $1,910,000.

($2,100,000 in rent paid less interest $190,000 = $1,910,000)

The third generation saved $2,720,000.

($2,940,000) in rent less interest $220,000 = $2,720,000)

Three generations of the Buyer family saved $5,789,000 when comparing rent to the cost of owning.

Note, the savings are actually greater since we are not considering the tax refunds due to being able to deduct interest on your tax return. If you were in a 28% tax bracket you would save an additional 28% of $5,789,000 or $1,620,920.

This information is a conservative indicator of values and how you and your family will create wealth through homeownership.

...*BUT* LET'S GO BACK TO OUR STORY.

These savings resulted from the Buyers deciding to purchase a home instead of renting.

The results speak for themselves: why would you rent if you can buy? Why create wealth for a landlord if you can create wealth for yourself? The funds saved or invested during their lifetime could have created additional wealth. It could be used for a better style of living, vacations, starting a business, sending the kids to a better school or college education, or investing in creating more wealth for your family.

Again, this is the wealth saved by buying a home and not renting. It is a small part of the wealth and opportunity of owning real estate. We still have to add in the wealth created by all 13 wealth creators. By working together and making sacrifices initially, this family can easily create millions of dollars in generational wealth, thus improving their community's lives and establishing a solid foundation for future generations. If they remained as tenants, however, they would have nothing to show for it but rent receipts.

Ownership may be a struggle at first, but it is not the lifelong struggle experienced by renters. Once you purchase a home, ownership gets easier yearly since the payment is the same, but incomes increase over time. Homeownership is (and should continue to be) the American dream. Homeownership starts with sacrifice; homeownership gets cheaper over time as incomes increase. Homeownership is America at its best, helping people improve their lives and the lives of their children.

OWNERS SCORECARD

The total amount saved by three generations of owners by buying and not renting was: $5,789,000 plus $1,620,920 in tax refunds.

RENTERS SCORECARD

The tenants have to pay rent as long as they live. The three generations considering _rent only_ have lost $6,228,000 and could have saved this if they had only purchased. _Remember_, this does not account for inflation adjusted rent pricing, lost appreciation, equity accumulation, and more; thus, this is a conservative figure.

WHAT WE HAVE LEARNED IN CHAPTER 4

1. We know the parents could have purchased a home for $25,000.

2. The total payment was $54,000 in principal and interest, with $25,000 paid in principal and $29,000 spent in interest.

3. The loan is paid off in 30 years with no mortgage payments after that, but rent lasts for as long as you are the tenant.

4. The grandparents saved $1,159,000 by buying.

5. Based on the son's rent, he could qualify for a mortgage of $350,000 with a payment of $1,500.

6. Total monthly payments on a mortgage over 30 years total are $540,000.

7. The principal paid was $350,000, and the amount of interest was $190,000.

8. The son saved $1,910,000 over his lifetime.

9. The rent paid by the grandson would finance $500,000. His total principal and interest paid over 30 years would be $720,000.

10. From the $720,000, subtract the principal paid $500,000, leaving interest paid at $220,000.

11. The rent saved over the grandson's lifetime was $2,720,000.

12. By buying and not renting, our three generations would save $5,789,000.

13. Being a homeowner takes some sacrifice but creates generational wealth and a better, more comfortable lifestyle.

14. The wealth created through ownership is much more remarkable when you add the wealth created by all 13 wealth creators.

15. Buying requires sacrifice, but the rewards are worth it. You may have to work two jobs for a few years, avoid going out much for lunch and dinners, and the list goes on, but the sacrifice justifies the benefits.

CHAPTER 5

RENT VS. BUY WORKSHEET

THE RENT VS. BUY WORKSHEET IS THE FOUNDATION ON WHICH WE WILL BUILD OUR PROGRAM FOR HOW TO CREATE WEALTH THROUGH REAL ESTATE

Reminder: *This is not a book about how to buy real estate, but rather* a study of how wealth is created in real estate and how you can accelerate the process of creating wealth for you and your family. On the following pages, you will see a typical rent vs. buy worksheet developed by my mother, Mary Savio, in 1960 to explain home ownership to renters. The explanation is based on comparing the cost of renting to the cost of buying. This worksheet is a simple way to explain the concept.

The two sample forms show first a blank form that is ready to be filled in with your data. The second form has been completed using an example of an affordable unit in Hawaii. It could be a unit in any neighborhood. This example will be used to compare the cost of renting to the cost of buying. The form is simple but also packed with information. The rent vs. buy worksheet will be the basis of our discussion and hopefully make it easier to follow.

Use the worksheet if you are thinking of buying a property.

Before continuing this chapter, we highly recommend you visit the www.savio.com/rentvsbuy or www.saviomanagement.com/rentvsbuy webpage, fill in your email, and get the complete set of worksheets. Print and continue through the book, as these will help facilitate your learning.

The purpose is to take a snapshot in time when tenants are considering buying a home, as this is an opportunity to explain the advantages of buying and compare renting vs. buying. After reading the book, you should be able to fill out the worksheet and get an idea of your rental cost compared to the cost of buying. You should also have a clear picture of real estate, how it creates wealth, and how you can use what you have learned to buy your first home or investment property. The knowledge and use of the worksheet will help you make the right decision. Our measuring stick will be the cost of renting and the savings created by ownership. This is accomplished by comparing the monthly costs for renting and buying. Renting usually appears cheaper than buying, so it is important to show all the savings and costs, and not just look at the monthly mortgage payments compared to rental payments. The benefits of ownership are what you want if you are the renter, and the wealth created passes to the landlord through rental payments.

As it turns out, the owner/buyer has certain advantages that reduce the actual purchase cost. The renter does not get the same advantages an owner/buyer does, so the renter loses those opportunities. This provides a true picture of the cost of renting. As you go through the chapter, you will see the advantage of ownership. Since rent is paid monthly and mortgage payments are also paid monthly, all numbers used should be done on a monthly basis. If property taxes or insurance are paid annually, convert the amounts to monthly numbers by dividing by 12 months.

You may know most of the information or be aware of it. Still, by not seeing it on the worksheet, you may not realize it or understand the relationship between the different components of the wealth creators.

Take a look at the forms. Understanding the rent vs. buy worksheet will be explained in the remaining chapters.

RENT VS. BUY WORKSHEET OWNER-OCCUPANT

RENT-VS-BUY WORKSHEET
OWNER-OCCUPANT

FOR: _____   DATE: _____

(A) PROPERTY DESCRIPTION		BUY	RENT
I. Description:	_____		
II. Location:	_____		
III. Land Tenure:	_____		
IV. Down Payment:	_____		
V. Financing Terms:	_____		
VI. Tax Assumptions:	_____		

(B) FINANCING TERMS		
1. Sales Price of Home	_____	
2. Cash Required for Down Payment	_____	
3. Mortgage	_____	
4. Other		

(C) MONTHLY PAYMENT		
5. Principal and Interest (P & I)		_____
(Line 5 – Line 11 = Principal)		
6. Deposit for Property Taxes (Approximate)		_____
7. Mortgage Insurance - Lender		_____
8. Maintenance Payments (AOUA)		_____
9. Other: _____		_____
10. Total Monthly Payments		_____

(D) ACTUAL MONTHLY TAX DEDUCTIBLE EXPENSES	
Homeowner's Tax Deductible Expenses	
11. First Month's Interest	_____
(Line 3 x Interest Rate ÷ 12 = Interest Per Month)	
12. Monthly Tax Deposit	_____
13. Mortgage Insurance	_____
14. Total Deductions	_____

(E) CASH SAVINGS PER MONTH ON TAXES	
(TAX BRACKET % x TOTAL DEDUCTIONS AS SHOWN ON LINE 12)	
15. 31% Tax Bracket ($____ x 31%) Line 14 x 31% =	_____
16. 28% Tax Bracket ($____ x 28%) Line 14 x 28% =	_____
17. 15% Tax Bracket ($___ x 15%) Line 14 x 15% =	_____

(F) DETERMINING ACTUAL MONTHLY COST OF BUYING (WHEN ADJUSTED FOR TAX & EQUITY PAID)

	31%	28%	15%		
18. Total Monthly Payment (Line 10)	_____	_____	_____		
19. Subtract Cash Savings on Taxes	_____	_____	_____		
(Line 15, Line 16, or Line 17)					
20. Monthly Payment Adjusted for Tax Savings	_____	_____	_____		
21. Subtract EQUITY Portion of Monthly Payment	_____	_____	_____		
(Equity or Principal = Line 5 Minus Interest x Line 11)					
22. Actual Monthly Payment	_____	_____	_____		
				What You Are Paying to Own	What You Are Paying to Rent

(G) DIFFERENT MONTHLY PAYMENTS BASED ON AMORTIZATION

Comparison of Payments and Amortization

	Payment Option 1: 30 Yr	Payment Option 2: 25 Yr	Difference Option 1	Payment Option 3: 20 Yr	Difference Option 1
Monthly Principal & Interest:					
x Term of Loan in Months					
"= Total Principal & Interest					
- Beginning Mortgage Balance					
"= Interest Paid					

RENT VS. BUY WORKSHEET OWNER-OCCUPANT FILLED OUT

RENT-VS-BUY WORKSHEET
OWNER-OCCUPANT

FOR: _____   DATE: _____

(A) PROPERTY DESCRIPTION		BUY	RENT
I. Description:	2-Bedroom /1-Bath		$ 1,200
II. Location:	Plantation Town Apartments		
III. Land Tenure:	Fee Simple		
IV. Down Payment:	20%		
V. Financing Terms:	1st Mortgage: 30-Year Mortgage / 5% Interest		
VI. Tax Assumptions:	Owner-Occupant Using Itemized Deductions		

(B) FINANCING TERMS		
1. Sales Price of Home	$	236,000
2. Cash Required for Down Payment	$	47,200
3. Mortgage	$	188,800
4. Other	$	-

(C) MONTHLY PAYMENT		
5. Principal and Interest (P & I)	$	1,014.00
(Line 5 - Line 11 = Principal)		
6. Deposit for Property Taxes (Approximate)	$	72.00
7. Mortgage Insurance - Lender		
8. Maintenance Payments (AOUO)	$	255.00
9. Other: _____	$	-
10. Total Monthly Payments	$ 1,341.00	$1200

(D) ACTUAL MONTHLY TAX DEDUCTIBLE EXPENSES		
Homeowner's Tax Deductible Expenses		
11. First Month's Interest	$	787
(Line 3 x Interest Rate / 12 = Interest Per Month)		
12. Monthly Tax Deposit	$	72
13. Mortgage Insurance		
14. Total Deductions	$	859

(E) CASH SAVINGS PER MONTH ON TAXES		
(TAX BRACKET % x TOTAL DEDUCTIONS AS SHOWN ON LINE 12)		
15. 31% Tax Bracket ($____ x 31%) Line 14 x 31% =	$	266
16. 28% Tax Bracket ($____ x 28%) Line 14 x 28% =	$	241
17. 15% Tax Bracket ($___ x 15%) Line 14 x 15% =	$	129

(F) DETERMINING ACTUAL MONTHLY COST OF BUYING (WHEN ADJUSTED FOR TAX & EQUITY PAID)	31%	28%	15%		
18. Total Monthly Payment (Line 10)	$ 1,341	$ 1,341	$ 1,341		
19. Subtract Cash Savings on Taxes					
(Line 15, Line 16, or Line 17)	$ 266	$ 241	$ 129		$ 241
20. Monthly Payment Adjusted for Tax Savings	$ 1,075	$ 1,100	$ 1,212		
21. Subtract EQUITY Portion of Monthly Payment					
(Equity or Principal = Line 5 Minus Interest x Line 11)	$ 227	$ 227	$ 227		$ 227
22. Actual Monthly Payment	$ 848	$ 873	$ 985		$ 1,668
				What You Are Paying to Own	What You Are Paying to Rent

(G) DIFFERENT MONTHLY PAYMENTS BASED ON AMORTIZATION					
Comparison of Payments and Amortization	Payment Option 1: 30 Yr	Payment Option 2: 25 Yr	Difference Option 1	Payment Option 3: 20 Yr	Difference Option 1
Monthly Principal & Interest:	$ 1,014	$ 1,104	$ 90	$ 1,246	$ 232
x Term of Loan in Months	360	300		240	
"= Total Principal & Interest	$ 365,040	$ 331,200		$ 299,040	
- Beginning Mortgage Balance	$ 188,800	$ 188,800		$ 188,800	
"= Interest Paid	$ 176,240	$ 142,400	$ 33,840	$ 110,240	$ 66,000

EXPLAINING THE WORKSHEET

The rent vs. buy worksheet is divided into seven sections: (A) through (G).

Section (A) covers the description of the property, and the assumptions made for financing and taxes.

(A)	PROPERTY DESCRIPTION		BUY	RENT
I.	Description:	2-Bedroom / 1-Bath		$1,200
II.	Location:	Plantation Town Apartments		
III.	Land Tenure:	Fee Simple		
IV.	Down Payment:	**20%**		
V.	Financing Terms:	1st Mortgage: 30-Year Mortgage / 5% Interest		
VI.	Tax Assumptions:	Owner-Occupant Using Itemized Deductions		

Lines A I, Description, and A II, Location

Prepare a separate form for two or three properties you like. This will help you consider the property based on the best potential to create wealth. Ultimately, you should buy a property based on what is best for your family, not solely on what is the best property for creating wealth. If the properties analyzed are equal in meeting your family's needs, then the choice may be the one that is better at creating wealth.

You will live in this home, so it must be right for you. As part of the purchase of a first home, you may have to make some sacrifices. If a home does not feel right for you and your family, it should not be purchased. Do not sacrifice your family's happiness. In fact, buying a home that does not work for you could be the reason for failure. Buy a property you will be happy to live in.

Line A III, Land Tenure

There are a number of different types of land tenure. We will focus only on Fee Simple and Leasehold.

Fee Simple is the highest form of property ownership. The owner has full control over the property and can sell, lease, or transfer it. This ownership is indefinite and typically passes to heirs upon death.

Leasehold is a property interest where the owner (the leaseholder) holds the right to use and occupy the improvements and the land for a specified period, according to a lease agreement, but does not own the land itself. The land reverts back to the landowner when the lease term ends. Hawaii has more residential leaseholds than any other market in the United States. Due, to land reform leasehold is a dying form of ownership in Hawaii.

Line A IV, Down Payment

Today (as of the time of writing this book), the average down payment is about 20%. VA loans offer 100% financing. Also, Section 8 rental voucher programs can be used to buy real estate. The Section 8 payment becomes a guaranteed income and should qualify for a no-money or low-down mortgage program. Ask your realtor if you have any questions about financing.

Line A V, Financing Terms

Financing is important, as the interest rate and term of the loan are needed to determine the monthly payment. The same financing is not always available for every property. Loans are usually available in 25, 30, and sometimes 40-year amortizations. It is recommended that you take the most extended term possible. You can simply pay additional amounts monthly to pay your loan off faster. Paying more monthly or in lump sums will reduce the term or length of the loan.

Line A VI, Federal and State Income Tax Assumptions

You should check with your realtor or tax consultant if you have concerns about your tax situation. We are not giving tax advice but rather are attempting to show the impact of income taxes on real estate ownership—especially in deciding whether to rent or purchase/buy.

Section (B) FINANCING TERMS

(B)	FINANCING TERMS	
1.	Sales Price of Home	$236,000
2.	Cash Required for Down Payment	$47,200
3.	Mortgage	$188,800
4.	Other	$ -

Lines 1–4. Most of the calculations in our journey through ownership will use this information as the foundation to quantify the cost and/or savings generated by ownership of a home or apartment.

Line 1: fill in the sales price.

Line 2: fill in the down payment.

Line 3: fill in the mortgage amount.

The down payment is always a concern for buyers. It is recommended that you investigate the following possibilities with your realtor:

IRA

Can you use any funds in your IRA or 401(k)?

If buying a home, you may be able to take up to $10,000 from your IRA without paying any penalty.

If married, each of you may be able to withdraw $10,000 from your IRA.

ROTH

You can borrow $10,000 each from your accounts without penalty if you have a ROTH IRA.

401(k)

If you have a 401(k), you can borrow $50,000 from an account to purchase a home without penalty.

You should talk to your realtor or tax consultant to understand the requirements of borrowing from an IRA or 401(k).

Check your local state and county to see if they have any down payment programs for first-time home buyers.

Section (C) MONTHLY PAYMENT

(C)	MONTHLY PAYMENT		
5.	Principal and Interest (P & I) (Line 5 - Line 11 = Principal)	$1,014.00
6.	Deposit for Property Taxes (Approximate)	$72.00
7.	Mortgage Insurance - Lender	$0.00
8.	Maintenance Payments (AOUA)	$255,00
9.	Other: _____	$0.00
10.	**Total Monthly Payments**	**$1,341.00**

Line 5. This is your monthly mortgage payment, which is determined by the interaction of the amortization or term of the loan and the amount borrowed or financed, as well as the interest rate you will be paying. Consult your realtor or lender or search the Internet for rates

and payments of the required loan balance, because the numbers will change due to amortization.

Line 6. This is the monthly property tax. Lenders usually require property taxes to be collected with your monthly mortgage and placed in a trust fund. The lender will pay the real property taxes when they are due. The lender may collect the fire and liability insurance with your monthly payment and make these payments to the insurance company when due. Insurance protects you and the lender from any insured losses.

Line 7. This is mortgage insurance, which will pay off the loan in case the borrower defaults on it. Lenders usually require it on loans with less than the normal down payment. You can verify with the lender that this insurance can be canceled once the equity reaches the standard 20% of the original sales price. It is best to avoid a loan that requires the insurance to remain for the term of the loan. The IRS has determined that mortgage insurance can be deducted as an interest expense for tax purposes.

To expand prior to continuing to Line 8: equity may reach 20% due to a paid principal or increase in the market value, whereby the insurance may be canceled. The benefit of this is that it permits the owner to save those funds and use them as additional principal payments to help reduce and pay back their loan faster and accelerate equity accumulation.

In fairness to the lender waving the mortgage insurance, the decision to release the need for insurance should be set at ownership, or the equity interest is greater than 20%. Remember, this may include appreciation. If the appreciation is a large part of the created value appreciation, this is a scenario where there may be a need for greater equity, then normally above 20%. This would protect the lender and the buyer if the majority of this increase were created by appreciation or inflation. However, if the equity is created from the paydown of the loan (that is, solid dollars that the buyer has put in), that should qualify for the mortgage insurance to be released once they hit the 20% equity. So, realize it is not just equity but how that equity was created when it comes to the lender's and insurance companies' decision to release mortgage insurance.

In summary, getting the insurance premium waived is also a reward for paying additional principal payments whenever possible. Continuing on...

Line 8. Suppose the property you are purchasing is a condominium or has a homeowners' or community association. In that case, there may be a monthly maintenance fee. As a rule, it includes fire and liability insurance, water, electricity, sewer, cable TV, internet, security, repairs, and replacement reserves. The costs to maintain a home and apartment are comparable. However, the payment method is different. Many people think a condominium is more expensive because of the maintenance fee, but in reality, homes have similar costs. A private homeowner does not set aside monthly reserves for painting, reroofing, etc. Private homeowners pay for these items when they must be done. A condominium requires owners to make monthly payments to a reserve account to ensure funds for these items are available when needed. On a per-unit basis, roofing, painting, etc. are cheaper in a condominium vs. a single-family home. Also, most utilities have significant user discounts, and condominiums should qualify for those savings.

If you buy a condominium unit, get involved, run for a position on the board, serve on a committee, etc., you have input and knowledge about your property.

Line 9. This is blank. Other expenses, if there are any, can be listed here.

Line 10. This is the total of all the costs paid monthly.

Section (D) MONTHLY TAX-DEDUCTIBLE EXPENSES

(D)	ACTUAL MONTHLY TAX-DEDUCTIBLE EXPENSES	
	Homeowner's Tax-Deductible Expenses	
11.	First Month's Interest	$787
	(Line 3 x Interest Rate / 12 = Interest Per Month)	
12.	Monthly Tax Deposit	$72
13.	Mortgage Insurance	
14.	**Total Deductions**	**$859**

Lines 11–14. These are the amounts of interest, property taxes, and mortgage insurance that can be deducted by a homeowner as expenses.

To compute interest for Line 11, the formula is:

Mortgage Balance $188,800

X Interest Rate of 5%

= $9,440 Annual interest

Annual Interest $9,440

/ by 12 months

= $787 Monthly Interest

Remember, this is the interest for the balances of the current month, shown in the example of $188,800 owed. So, that balance after the first payment is $188,573. For...

Principal & Interest $1,014

- $787 Interest

= $227 Principal

Then...

Mortgage Balance $188,800

- $227 Principal

= $188,573 Remaining Principal

Interest for next month will be a little lower, and the principal will go up by the exact amount interest went down.

For Lines 12 and 13, transfer the information from Lines 6 and 7 (real property taxes and mortgage insurance).

Section (E) COMPUTATION OF MONTHLY TAX SAVINGS

(E)	CASH SAVINGS PER MONTH ON TAXES	
	(TAX BRACKET % x TOTAL DEDUCTIONS AS SHOWN ON LINE 14)	
15.	31% Tax Bracket ($859 x 31%) Line 14 x 31% =	$266
16.	28% Tax Bracket ($859 x 28%) Line 14 x 28% =	$241
17.	15% Tax Bracket ($859 x 15%) Line 14 x 15% =	$129

Lines 15, 16, and 17. These represent the monthly tax savings assuming different tax brackets. A client can then choose the one that is closest to his actual tax bracket. Remember that this form is designed to compare renting vs. ownership and does not provide a detailed analysis of taxes. To compute the taxes owed for the various tax brackets, take the information in Line 14 and multiply it by the percentages shown in 15, 16, and 17.

Section (F) DETERMINING ACTUAL MONTHLY COST OF BUYING (when adjusted for Tax & Equity)

Lines 18–23. We now determine the actual cost of buying vs. renting. To do this, we fill in Line 18 by taking the total monthly payment shown in Line 10. Then, fill in Line 19 with the appropriate tax savings from Lines 15, 16, and 17. Next, subtract Line 19 from Line 18. This gives you the total payment less tax savings.

(F)	DETERMINING ACTUAL MONTHLY COST OF BUYING				
		31%	28%	15%	
18.	Total Monthly Payment (Line 10)	$1,341	$1,341	$1,341	
19.	Subtract Cash Savings on Taxes				
	(Line 15, Line 16, or Line 17)	$266	$241	$129	$241
20.	Monthly Payment Adjusted for Tax Savings	$1,075	$1,100	$1,212	
21.	Subtract EQUITY Portion of Monthly Payment				
	(Equity or Principal = Line 5 Minus Interest x Line 11)	$227	$227	$227	$227
22.	**Actual Monthly Payment**	**$848**	**$873**	**$985**	
					What You Are
					Paying to Rent

The next step is to compute the principal paid monthly on the loan used in the example. To compute that from Line 5, principal and interest, subtract Line 11, which is the first month's interest.

Line 5 (Principal & Interest) $1,014

- Line 11 (First Month's Interest) $787

= Line 21 (Equity Portion of Monthly Payment) $227

This balance remaining is the principal. In this example, it is $227, which is entered on Line 21. Remember that the principal payment of $227 is deducted from the balance owed, so debt is reduced from $188,800 to $188,573. The second-month interest is computed on a new balance.

We then subtract the amount on Line 21 (which is the principal payment) from the balance on Line 20. Line 22 is the adjusted cost of buying the home after savings are subtracted. In our examples, it ranges from $848 to $985 depending on your tax tier.

Line 20 (Monthly Payment Adjusted for Tax Savings) $1,075

- Line 21 (Equity Portion of the Monthly Payment) $227

= Line 22 (Actual Monthly Payment) $848 to $985

The actual cost of buying has decreased since the buyer will get a refund from federal and state taxes (however, some states do not have state income taxes). The tax deductions reduce monthly payments. The same is valid with the principal because it is not a cost of buying, but rather a saving due to ownership you get back when you refinance or sell. The original payment or monthly cost of the home was $1,341 per month. The actual cost to buy the home is only $873 in the 28% tax bracket per month after adjustments. This shows that ownership appeared to be more expensive originally than renting but owning is cheaper than renting if you understand real estate.

To summarize, you as a buyer pay $1,341 but get back taxes and interest. Or, in another way, your monthly payment is $1,341 but the principal payment is yours, as it reduces the principal amount owed. The tax savings due to interest (which can include mortgage insurance premiums) are paid as a refund at the end of the year in the form of a tax refund.

Thus, you pay the full amount of $1,341, but after accounting for the principal portion paid and the tax refund back, the actual monthly cost shown in Line 22 is considerably less; as we see in our example, it ranges between $848, $873, and $985.

To me, this information is important since you are sacrificing to make the payment; at least you know it is coming back to you over time. It also means that if you rent for $1,200, you can pay more because you get financial benefits as an owner, while as a tenant, you get none and pay more in taxes.

Later, we will go over other savings that can further reduce the effective monthly cost (and even the actual month-to-month cost), improving cash flow.

HOW DOES THE RENTER COMPARE TO THE BUYER?

A renter pays rent twice; they pay rent to the landlord but also pay rent in the form of higher taxes since they do not get the interest deduction and lose the principal paid monthly. So, the renter has a lower monthly cost of $1,200 compared to ownership of $1,341. The renter loses the benefits of ownership, so he actually pays more than the rent. The buyer is "paying" more than the tenant but gets the benefits of ownership.

Let's look at the rental side of the form. The market rent is $1,200, while the cost of buying was $1,341. At this point, renting looks cheaper than buying. A few adjustments must be made to the renter's side to balance the comparison of renting vs. owning.

We must add as a cost the advantages the tenant paid for by paying the rent but did not receive, along with the financial benefits created by renting that are paid for by the tenant but go to the owner, not the tenant. The tenant created a financial benefit for the landlord by paying the rent. The tenant pays for them but loses the advantage of the benefits since they are not the owner of the property. By making these adjustments, we get an idea of the actual cost of renting.

First, we must add back the tax savings (Line 19) using the 28% tax bracket; the tax savings is $241 (Line 19). In this case, the savings went to the landlord, not the tenant. Thus, it is a cost to the tenant. Since interest is tax-deductible, Uncle Sam allows the owner to deduct it as an expense, reducing their tax liability. In this case, the tenant is paying rent to the landlord, and the landlord gets a tax refund of $241 per month.

19.	Subtract Cash Savings on Taxes				
	(Line 15, Line 16, or Line 17)	$266	$241	$129	$241

The tenant paid the owner's interest on the loan by renting, but the tenant got none of the benefits. Thus, they paid the interest but lost the tax refund of $241. So, the tenant pays his rent twice—once to the landlord and an additional $241 to the federal government. At this point, the tenant's rent cost is not $1,200 but is, in fact, $1,441.

Monthly Rent of $1,200

+ Owner Interest Deduction of $241 a month

= $1,441

When paying rent, the tenant pays the landlord's mortgage, so the tenant also pays the principal on the landlord's loan. The tenant pays it, but the owner gets the benefit. Line 21 shows the principal that is paid. That $227 is paid by the tenant, but he receives no benefit, so it is a cost to him. The renter's cost payment is not $1,441. The actual cost to rent is $1,668. As seen in the calculation below.

Monthly Rent of $1,200

+ Owner Interest Deduction of $241 a month

+ Owner Principal of $227 a month

= $1,668

(*Note:* the above benefits of $241 and $227 could have gone to the tenant if they were the owner.)

The owner gets a tax deduction, and the renter pays higher taxes. The owner receives his mortgage paid off by the tenant, and the tenant pays rent forever.

We did not add an amount to represent the renters' loss of the potential of owners' appreciation (increase in home value), which could easily be 3% to 5% of the previous year's value.

That would be $7,080 to $11,800 in the first year on a $236,000 purchase price. That is a further reduction in the cost of owning compared to renting at $850 to $1,250 per month. It's a cost for renters since you give that value to your landlord.

Let's use the more conservative $7,080 a year in appreciation.

The actual cost and opportunity cost lost by the tenant are as follows:

From all indications, buying a home makes more sense, and renting is *sneakily* more expensive than you realize. The family that rents is giving away its wealth and its potential to the landlord. They are creating the same potential and value as ownership, but it is not theirs to keep. Renting is a process that transfers value from the tenant to the owner/landlord. Renting is not something you should deliberately do to your family.

Understanding this simple comparison is why we should strive for home ownership. That is why we should encourage our government to support homeownership for all tenant-owned apartment buildings. As a throwback to my first release, *Hawaii's Housing Solution, "Move to the Mainland": 60 Years of Failure, IT MUST END*; it is discussed in that book that government housing programs should strive to eliminate landlord-owned rentals and support tenant ownership. In a tenant-owned building, mortgage payments stay constant for 30 years. This will stabilize broader market rents and the tenant's cost of living as to housing. The building's mortgage is paid off, and the tenant's costs will decline as if he were the owner, giving him ownership advantages. I digress... let's continue.

THE TOTAL COST FOR THE OWNER

The homeowner's cost was $1,341. In addition to rent, the owner gets $468 back ($241 in tax refund and $227 in principal). Remember, I left the appreciation out of the calculation. The actual cost of ownership (not including appreciation) is $873. Again, understanding real estate makes ownership easier.

Including appreciation at 3%, the owner's cost would go down to $283 a month, or at 5%, the owner's expense to own the home would go down to $110 per month. Keep in mind, the owner-investor will cost a total of $1,341 for the home each month while earning $1,200 in rent. However, with the benefits of ownership, the owner's actual "cost" will be $283 to $110 a month. For the owner-investor, they get the former plus rents and additional deductions.

Owner Payment $1,341
($1,014 Principal & Interest, $72 Property Tax, $255 Maintenance Fee)

-$468 ($241 Tax Refund & $227 Principal)

-$590 Earned 3% Appreciation

= $238 true cost a month OR $110 a month if at 5% Appreciation

THE TOTAL COST FOR THE RENTER

Rent is not a cost of $1,200 but actually costs the tenant $1,668 (not including appreciation of 3% to 5% if added); it would increase the cost by (3%) $590 to $983 per month, increasing the cost to $2,258 to $2,651.

Again...

Monthly Rent of $1,200

+ Owner Interest Deduction of $241 a month

+ Owner Principal of $227 a month

+ Loss of Possible Appreciation of $590 a month (at 3%)

= $2,258 or $2,651 if at 5% Appreciation

Renting became more expensive than owning. Owning is nearly free or (in some scenarios) free after all advantages are accounted for.

If they had purchased the home, it would have cost $1,314.

However, with the benefits of ownership, it would cost only $873 to buy after the principal was paid and tax savings (with no appreciation). If you include appreciation, the cost would be nearer to zero—but in some scenarios, it would be less than zero. However, I do not usually include appreciation since it is a value that is typically collected sometime in the future when the house is sold.

As we can see, the renter is giving the benefits away to the owner.

WHAT WE HAVE LEARNED IN CHAPTER 5

1. We learned how to fill out the rent vs. buy worksheet.

2. We learned how the form helps us standardize our review and compare properties based on financial assumptions.

3. The rent vs. buy worksheet is broken down into six sections.

4. Those six sections are:

    i.   Section A covers information on property.

    ii. Section B contains information on financing.

    iii. Section C shows the total monthly payment and what is included. Mortgage insurance in Section C is not life insurance, but the insurance charged by lenders when they accept a low-down payment loan. Insurance guarantees a down payment if there's a default.

    iv. Sections D & E deal with taxes and equity growth.

    v.   Section F shows the actual cost of buying after deductions for the benefit of ownership.

    vi. Section G represents the interest that can be saved by increasing principal payments or reducing amortization.

5. Maintenance fees refer to condos and homeowners' associations, if applicable.

6. Interest, property tax, and lender mortgage insurance are tax deductible.

7. We were introduced to the formula for computing yearly interest: amount owed/borrowed/mortgage balance x interest rate = annual interest.

8. Computing monthly interest; yearly interest divided by 12 months = monthly interest.

9. Lines 15, 16, and 17 show possible monthly tax savings using different tax rates: low, medium, and high.

10. You must have cash for the down payment and/or closing costs to buy.

11. The cash requirements are one of the biggest challenges for buyers.

12. If you are a first-time buyer, you should interview and find a realtor in your area, you can work with—hopefully one who has read the book and understands the concepts.

13. The realtor fee is usually paid by the seller, and it is in the price of the home, so don't think you will save money by not having a realtor. You want someone representing and helping you through the process.

14. Section 8 rental vouchers can be used to buy property.

15. If Section 8, the government will guarantee you a voucher for up to 15 years to help you buy a home.

16. When looking at a mortgage or the amount you need to borrow, always show the loan amount, the term in years, and the interest rate.

17. The combination of the loan needed, interest rate, and term of maturity will determine the monthly principal and interest payment.

18. I always recommend the 30-year amortization even if the 15-year is cheaper because the 30-year payment is lower. You buy a home, but you also lock in and agree to a payment. If you pay more monthly, you can pay a 30-year term off sooner.

19. Amortization is not as important because we teach and assume everyone will pay off their loan in 10 to 15 years regardless of the original amortization by following the wealth creators and approach championed. However, we will be covering its magic later because it is often misunderstood.

20. Loans are usually amortized for 15, 25, 30, or 40 years. If 40-year amortization is available, it should be the lowest payment. Just take it.

21. Any additional payment, whether in bulk (a tax refund, gift, bonus, or inheritance) or a small amount paid monthly, will be credited to the principal automatically and reduce the term of the loan.

22. A mortgage payment should be around ⅓ of your income.

23. The amount you can borrow is related to your income and other expenses.

24. In addition to income, a lender will look at the length of employment and your credit history.

25. Lenders are looking at your ability to repay over a long period of time—employment stability.

26. Lenders' mortgage insurance may be required if you buy with a low-down payment.

27. Lenders' mortgage insurance insures lenders for low-down payment risk. It does not insure you, the borrower. If you want buyers' mortgage life insurance to protect your family if you should die, you need to buy it from your insurance agent.

28. Lenders' mortgage insurance premiums are considered additional interest and can be deducted as an investor lender when computing income taxes.

29. Mortgage insurance can be canceled once equity reaches 20% equity. If you can cancel mortgage insurance, cancel it, but do not reduce the monthly payment. That extra amount that was paid will go to the principal once you are able to cancel insurance and continue making that extra payment amount. It will be credited as an additional principal payment, saving you interest going forward.

30. Appreciation can go up, but it can also go down. If using appreciation above the purchase price to cancel mortgage insurance, the lender may want to see more than 20% equity. This empha-

sizes the sacrifice of waiting for appreciation and the effort required to make additional payments to achieve similar equity levels.

31. Suppose you take my advice and pay the additional principal. That is the equivalent of putting more down since you put in the money monthly. Lenders should give you 100% of that amount toward equity to stop the need for mortgage insurance.

32. Condominiums have maintenance fees, and people who don't understand often complain about the high fees. However, in a well-managed building, common expenses should be lower than the cost of an individual home.

33. Condominiums often qualify for lower bulk rates on electricity, water and sewer fees, cable, internet, TV, and insurance.

34. Condo maintenance fees confuse people into believing they are high because increases come yearly. Single-family homes get larger increases throughout the year, so it's not noticed as much.

35. Also, single-family units do not set aside monthly monies for major repairs and replacements of roofs and plumbing, but condos do.

36. If you are buying a condo, get involved, go to board meetings, and volunteer to be on any committees that need help and run for the board.

37. If you have questions about condos or maintenance fees, ask your realtor; they can help find the answer or send you to the person who can help.

38. The loan balance goes down monthly as payments on the principal are made. The total monthly payment stays the same, only the allocation of principal and interest changes. Interest goes down every month, and since a portion of the loan is paid back, the principal goes up by the amount of interest saved. Saving is

the interest not paid to the lender since a portion of the original loan was paid down through the magic of amortization.

39. A lower total mortgage balance is owed to the lender. When interest is computed on the new lower debt balance following the following month, the interest will be lower. This will happen every month till the loan is paid off.

40. In determining the monthly interest, you always use the current balance.

41. Interest on the loan, property tax and mortgage insurance are tax-deductible.

42. Your rent is always higher than what you pay the landlord.

43. Using an estimated appreciation of 3% to 5% can significantly reduce the cost of buying. However, we typically don't factor it into the rent-to-buy comparison for appreciation, which is a future value that can fluctuate with the market, making it less predictable. Instead, we will focus on actual monthly payments and savings. Although this conservative approach may not account for potential appreciation, as you can see, it further advocates for and strengthens a robust case for buying over renting.

CHAPTER 6

RENT VS. BUY WORKSHEET SHOWING WEALTH CREATORS

A QUICK LOOK AT THE RENT VS. BUY WORKSHEET WITH WEALTH CREATORS IDENTIFIED

n the rent vs. buy worksheet, we show where the wealth creators are and how they are represented. You can clearly see the wealth creators in bold and underlined on the worksheet, have added arrows on the following sheets as well to clearly identify them. I will explain them in detail in the coming chapters.

Here is a snippet of the form (the complete form can be found in the back of the book as well):

(A)	PROPERTY DESCRIPTION		
I.	Description:	_____	**(2) Not Paying Rent (Refer to "DI." Below)**
II.	Location:	_____	
III.	Land Tenure:	Fee Simple	
IV.	Down Payment:	_____%	

V.	Financing Terms:	1st Mortgage: ___-Year Mortgage / __% Interest	
VI.	Tax Assumptions:	Owner-Occupant Using Itemized Deductions	
(B)	**FINANCING TERMS**		
	1. Purchase Price		**(3) Appreciation**
	2. Down Payment		**(4) Leverage**
	3. Mortgage		**(5) Savings Account**
	4. Other		

It is important to realize they are present in every real estate purchase. They will work automatically for you and your family every day you own real estate, creating value, wealth, and a better future.

Understanding them will help explain why becoming a homeowner is important to you and your family's future and can accelerate the creation of wealth through real estate ownership.

Knowledge will also give you more confidence about real estate and make your first purchase easier. It will help give you a clear path forward in creating a better, more rewarding life for you and your family.

You will also be more comfortable with taking on the responsibility of owning your own home. Additionally, understanding mortgage debt will give you confidence and comfort in taking on the responsibility of a mortgage.

Real estate debt can be your best friend.

Let's now look at the nine wealth creators in residential real estate.

IDENTIFYING THE WEALTH CREATORS IN REAL ESTATE

A brief description of them would be:

1. TIME - the first wealth creator. Time is represented by the date the search for a property to buy starts. Everything going forward will begin with that date. It is a reminder that we are looking over a long period of time (in our examples, we look at 60 years). It also represents patience, not rushing into a purchase. Think and plan your moves, and educate yourself about real estate.

2. NOT PAYING RENT - the second wealth creator is represented by the rent being paid today. Rent increases over time, as our earlier example shows. If you buy, rent stops and the mortgage payment can be set for 30 years with no change; when the loan is paid off, no mortgage payments need to be made. The money that went to the rent increases or the mortgage can now go to you and your family.

3. APPRECIATION - the third wealth creator. The starting point is the acquisition price. Over time, the value of real estate increases. It may stay flat or decrease in value, or increase and decrease in a serpentine fashion, but real estate will increase in value over time. That increase is called *"appreciation."* Historically, appreciation has been in the 3% to 5% range.

4. SAVINGS ACCOUNT, CALLED "MORTGAGE" - the fourth wealth creator. The original loan balance is the starting point. It represents the amount to be saved over time by the owner, who makes monthly principal payments.

5. LEVERAGE - the fifth wealth creator. Represented by the down payment and how debt increases our return. Leverage allows us to control a larger valuable asset or real estate by putting a small

amount of the total price as a down payment. The down payment typically ranges from 3% to 20%, and there is no money down on VA loans.

6. CONSTANT MONTHLY PAYMENT - the sixth wealth creator. It is represented by your mortgage payment, which comprises principal and interest. The payment remains the same for the loan term. If you have a 30-year term on your loan, the mortgage payment (unlike rent) remains the same for 30 years till the loan is paid off. On the other hand, rent goes up often and continues forever. Housing is the largest component of our cost of living. Ownership locks in that cost for the term of the loan—usually 30 years.

7. TAX SAVINGS - the seventh wealth creator. It represents the refunds that state and federal governments give to encourage home ownership. Interest and property taxes, which are included in the rent paid by a tenant or the monthly payment paid by an owner, are a big part of the deduction. The owner pays but gets a deduction and tax savings. The tenant receives no refund and pays more taxes compared to a buyer. For renters, they pay rent twice. They pay rent to the landlord and the government in the form of higher taxes.

8. PRINCIPAL PAID - the eighth wealth creator. It is the principal portion of the monthly mortgage payment that reduces debt. The principal goes to pay off the loan. It is a forced savings account created by the obligation to pay a monthly mortgage.

9. PREPAYMENTS - the ninth wealth creator. Any amount paid in addition to the established monthly payment; this can be an increase in payment monthly or a lump sum payment. Prepayments reduce the total amount of interest paid over the term of the loan and reduce the length or term of the loan. Following the book's advice, a 30-year loan can quickly be paid off in 10 years.

The key is understanding the wealth creators, which we will discuss in the coming chapters. You will want to understand them, learn how to take care of them, and work with them so that you can create wealth faster. The wealth creators will improve your life and the life of your family. You will create a better community, and you will set an example for your children and grandchildren to follow.

Renting gives away the opportunity to create and keep wealth.

Ownership gives you the opportunity to keep the wealth created by real estate.

This is a life-changing moment, and I hope reading this book will help you start looking seriously at buying a home and stopping renting. If you already own a home, I hope the knowledge will help you accelerate and support the wealth creators in improving your life.

Homeownership is about creating wealth and opportunity for you and your family.

WHAT WE HAVE LEARNED IN CHAPTER 6

1. This is not a book about how to buy real estate. It is a book that will help you buy by showing you how real estate works to create wealth. It will give you the knowledge and confidence to buy a home.

2. The rent vs. buy worksheet compares the cost of renting to the cost of ownership.

3. The structure of the book is based on the rent vs. buy worksheet, showing a family that rents and what could happen if they had purchased.

4. We also identified the wealth creators and their location on the worksheet.

5. Wealth creators are structured into the process and will work by themselves.

6. Knowing the wealth creators gives you knowledge about real estate and why purchasing is important.

7. Knowing the wealth creators gives you the confidence to buy.

8. Knowing the wealth creators will give you the knowledge to accelerate their creation for you and your family.

9. This book is about creating wealth for you and your family.

10. I am not teaching something most of you don't already have some knowledge of; I am simply putting it all together in one book on how you create value and a future by buying real estate.

11. Renting is a process where you create value but give it away to your landlord.

CHAPTER 7

MEET THE FIRST TWO WEALTH CREATORS

Remember, there are nine wealth creators in residential real estate. You must understand all of them so that you can accelerate the process and set realistic goals. As we go through our study of renting vs. buying, we will show the potential of the nine residential wealth creators embedded in real estate ownership. We will also see how your family could easily become multimillionaires over their lifetime simply by buying a home instead of renting.

This book is not about money, but rather about creating a better life. We use money or wealth as the measuring stick to determine the impact of the concepts discussed.

The wealth creators in real estate are a good force in homeownership. They allow (and are) the wealth creation process that is built into ownership of real estate. They are available to everyone who buys. There is no discrimination; you just need to have the knowledge and the desire to create a better life for you and your family.

INTRODUCING THE FIRST CREATOR OF WEALTH: "TIME"

This chapter introduces you to the first and second wealth creators.

Time is the first wealth creator.

Real estate is a long-term commitment. If you are buying to flip or re-sale immediately, you are not investing. You are operating a high-risk business; it is not investing in real estate. In this type of buy and flip program, you are a speculator. A small change in the market or interest rates can wipe out your equity.

In my program, everyone needs housing in the form of rental or ownership. I am encouraging ownership, showing the wealth created by ownership compared to renting.

You are looking at the wealth created throughout your life. This is not a "get rich quick" scheme; instead, it is a practical, well-thought-out, and deliberate plan for using the wealth creators in real estate to create wealth for you and your family.

We were introduced to time in terms of a lifetime (in our examples, a 60-to-70-year term). We then showed the advantage of time if you were to buy at 20 or 30 years old.

While wealth is created over time, time can have other advantages in real estate.

You may need time to save the down payment or improve your credit. You need time to learn how real estate works and creates value. It does not always need to be a lifetime. It may be a few months or a few years. The key is time to plan. That is the foundation for success in using real estate to create wealth. It is time that creates value and opportunity to build wealth.

So, OUR FIRST CREATOR OF WEALTH IN REAL ESTATE IS TIME.

THE SECOND CREATOR OF WEALTH IN REAL ESTATE: "NOT PAYING RENT"

You see this wealth creator clearly in the three-generational family. Not paying rent created $5,789,000 in savings for the family. That value does not include the additional wealth that could have been made by investing the money saved in real estate, stocks, bonds, other securities, collectibles, or alternative assets.

The cost of rent is forever. The cost of buying is limited to the term of the loan, but the savings for the homeowner and the creation of wealth are forever.

We explained it in the opening chapters using common sense and basic math. There is no question that buying made the most sense.

Remember, rent can go up every year as wages go up. However, ownership locks in a constant monthly payment, so the pay raise does not go to the landlord in the form of higher rent but stays with you to create more wealth. You pay rent for a lifetime but a mortgage for a specified period, and that payment is set for 30 years with no increase. It is better than rent.

At this point, we have only used the first two wealth creators, with seven more to go.

The actual potential wealth is much greater for our imaginary family, with only two wealth creators being identified. Use the knowledge to your advantage to create a better life and opportunities, invest in a business, or retire early.

The list of available options is yours to dream.

WHAT WE HAVE LEARNED IN CHAPTER 7

1. There are nine wealth creators in residential real estate.

2. Understanding the wealth creators will allow you to accelerate the creation of wealth.

3. Understanding will also give you the confidence to buy now.

4. Simply by buying a home, a family could become millionaires.

5. The first creator of wealth was time.

6. Wealth can be created throughout your lifetime.

7. You can use time to save money and plan your investment strategy.

8. Wealth creators are not a "get rich quick" scheme, but a deliberate plan to develop wealth over time by understanding and using them.

9. The second creator of wealth is not paying rent over your lifetime.

10. Mortgages are paid off in 15 to 30 years, and no payment is required.

11. Rent goes up with inflation.

12. Mortgage payments stay constant till the loan is paid in full.

13. Renting is paid for as long as you live.

14. Our family saved $5,789,000, and we still have seven more wealth creators to discover.

15. Now is the time to seriously consider buying.

CHAPTER 8

THE THIRD WEALTH CREATOR: APPRECIATION

O n our worksheet, appreciation is represented by the home's purchase price. In this example, for appreciation, let's use the same family that purchased a home in 1960 for $25,000.

Today, that home would easily sell for $700,000 to $1,000,000.

The appreciation or increase in value is the difference between the two prices. In this case, which comes out to $675,000 or $975,000.

Today's value is $700,000 to $1,000,000.

Original price: $25,000.

Appreciation: $675,000 to $975,000.

APPRECIATION

The simple definition is the increase in value of an asset over time.

The appreciated value belongs to the owner of the property, whether they be an owner-occupant or an investor/landlord who rents the home out.

As an owner, you did not have to do anything to create this value. It just happened due to the actions of the economic marketplace and government that create inflation and market demand, which increase values.

You can see the huge difference between home values in 1960 and 2024.

Remember, wages also went up in 1960.

In our example, $700 to $900 was the salary needed to buy the home. In 1960, that was the combined salary of a husband and wife working.

Cars, food, electricity, etc. were all a lot cheaper in the 1960s compared to today.

So, just owning a real estate asset, home, or condominium apartment can result in an increase in value over time. All you have to do is own it.

Appreciation is the third wealth creator.

The starting point is the price we paid, and the appreciation is all the value that gets added to our purchase price when we sell the property.

APPRECIATION MONTHLY

It may help when buying real estate; remember, you are financing a portion and paying a small down payment or only needing cash to cover closing costs if you use 100% financing.

The real estate you purchase is also increasing in value. It happens unnoticed by most owners until years later when the property's increase is seen by comparable properties selling at a higher price. This unnoticed increase in value due to appreciation helps to offset the cost of your monthly interest cost.

Today, real estate is appreciating at about 3% to 5% per year. That means, in our earlier example, a $236,000 home also increases in value by 3% annually. That comes out to $7,080 per year, or $590 per month.

The formula for computing the $ value of appreciation is:

Unit's value x inflation rate = inflation value per year

$236,000 x 3% = $7,080 Yearly

Appreciation Div. months = monthly appreciation amount

$7,080 divided by 12 = $590 per month

Again, we don't like to pay interest, but if we need financing to buy, we must pay the lender's interest.

The increase in value or appreciation is tax-free. So, we are offsetting the interest expense or outflow of funds for our mortgage payment by the tax-free growth or increase in value caused by appreciation.

In addition, the interest expense and property tax paid are tax deductible, so that amount is coming back as a tax refund due to the interest and property taxes being tax-deductible.

In this case, through appreciation, we are getting back another $590 per month plus the tax refund on interest and property taxes of $241.

Owner Property Tax & Interest Deduction of $241 a month

+ Appreciation of 3% $590 a month

= $831 a month of value accumulated & saved

*Note: this does not include principal paid.

So, we are getting back a total savings of $831 per month. We are paying $787 in interest. In reality, for this example, we are paying interest, but we are getting back more value through appreciation than the interest paid. You will find in most examples that you will pay little to no net interest when buying a home. Also, remember this does not account for the principal paid either. However, we will discuss the savings created monthly by paying the principal.

With this in mind, thinking you don't want to buy a home because interest is expensive is inaccurate. If you pay rent, you do not get anything back because it generates nothing, while if you pay to buy a home, you get money back as a deduction and tax refund at the end of the year. Buying pays you; renting will always cost you. When renting, you are paying your landlord's interest on his loan, but you never get it back. The landlord and his family receive the benefits, and the tenant pays the expense. So, everyone is paying interest (both the renter and the owner), but only the owner gets the benefits back.

You have to love home ownership. It is full of little surprises, and there are more to come.

Additionally, if interest rates go up, that usually means inflation goes up as well, so your appreciation keeps up with the increase in inflation. As interest rates go up, they also put downward pressure on values. So, interest rate increases could cause monthly payments to rise for new buyers, making it more challenging to buy, and could cause real estate values to slow, flatten, or even decline over time for all owners—even though over time, values go up.

It is possible that appreciation could stop (and even decline) but remember the wealth creator called "time"; maybe we should also add "patience" to the wealth creator of time. Over TIME and with PATIENCE, values will correct themselves and work to create the same wealth in different ways.

You have locked in a low mortgage payment for 30 years if you have purchased a home before interest rates have increased. You are in a good position and can wait. In our example of a family, the market went up over their lifetime, declined, and then continued an up-and-down increase and loss in value. Still, over long periods after the fluctuations, time shows a significant increase in value.

Eventually, inflation could cause faster and more significant pay raises, which means higher incomes and higher rents if you are not an owner. If you're already an owner, your employment income goes up. Still, the monthly housing costs remain constant, so the savings from owner-ship compared to renting are real.

As a homeowner, you can also use pay raises to pay off debt faster.

- ❖ Remember, real estate exists to create wealth for the owner. YOU WANT TO BE AN OWNER.
- ❖ Real estate takes value from the tenant. YOU DON'T WANT TO BE A TENANT!

HELPING APPRECIATION WORK FOR YOU

You can increase the value of your home further or faster by being strategic. Adding a patio or bedroom can upgrade the property, as you are adding or creating more appreciation. Keeping the present house and yard in excellent condition will increase desirability and price.

Being active in your neighborhood, your children's school, and your church creates a community and a better place to live, as well as more value through appreciation.

Further, involvement in politics (even just going to hearings, voting, etc.) helps create value. Good government and school districts make the area more desirable, so more people want to live there, and thus demand increases value.

As an owner, you should strive to stimulate appreciation and not just accept the appreciation that comes your way due to time.

You must realize that properties can lose value or depreciate if the home, school, or neighborhood deteriorates.

Be a positive influence, working with your neighbor and your community to be the best you can be and make your community the best it can be.

As to the value created by appreciation, renting has no comparable advantage. The effect of inflation on rents is an increase in rents. So, inflation contributes to the creation of appreciation, which is of value to the owner.

Inflation increases rents, which is also a benefit for the landlord/owner.

Rents go up with inflation, but mortgage payments stay the same, making buying more stable.

If renting, inflation increases all costs (including rent), and the tenant has to pay more. Inflation definitely hurts renters. Inflation helps owners, however, as discussed above.

So, in this case (and as it is with most wealth creators), the value goes to the owners, not the renter. Over the 60 years, the house in our original example increased in value 27 times above its original purchase price.

This indicates that today's values will also increase similarly over time.

So, the renter gets no value for appreciation, and the owner receives full value.

For the $25,000 property, that is $675,000 in appreciation on the low end.

The first two wealth creators are working quietly, and the owner is way ahead in creating value. Now, we add the value of the third wealth creator and the owner's position improves, whereas the renter's position weakens.

When comparing renting to owning, it could be said that RENTERS PAY AND OWNERS RECEIVE.

WHAT WE HAVE LEARNED IN CHAPTER 8

1. Appreciation is an increase in the value of an asset over time.

2. 60 years ago, a house that is $700,000 today would have cost $25,000 brand new. So, the house appreciated by $675,000. That same $700,000 house today could be $18,000,000 in 60 years.

3. Inflation has caused prices and wages to increase.

4. We learned to compute or determine the dollar value of appreciation.

5. Take the value of the house today and subtract the original purchase price. The increase in value is called "appreciation."

6. For an owner, inflation increases the value of an asset. For renters, inflation increases rent, which is a cost to the tenant.

7. "Renters pay" and "owners receive."

8. Owners can help increase the value of their property by adding to the home (such as more rooms, a patio, a pool, etc.).

9. Owners can also help increase the value of their homes through being involved in the community and schools.

10. Mortgage payments stay constant, and rent can increase.

11. Inflation increases all costs, including rent.

12. Your home is going up in value over time. That increase in value is yours to use in a myriad of ways for buying the property. It is one of the benefits of ownership.

CHAPTER 9

THE FOURTH WEALTH CREATOR: LEVERAGE

L EVERAGE is the concept of using other people's funds to increase your return or profit. It is the fourth wealth creator, and is represented by your down payment and mortgage debt, which equals the purchase price and the starting point for leverage.

Real estate leverage is the use of debt to increase the value or the amount you can pay when buying a home. In real estate, the debt is usually a first mortgage.

Real estate is one of the few investments that allows for relatively stable, safe, and easily available leverage through long-term financing.

Stocks and bonds may allow leverage by enabling purchases on margins, but this is riskier since a decline in the value of the stock could require immediate prepayment of the leverage advanced on value.

Real estate loans are long-term commitments by the lender (usually 15 to 30 years) that create long-term opportunities to generate value and thus magnify value and opportunity for increased growth or return on the assets. A long-term loan also provides you with stability.

Unlike in the stock market, real estate has no immediate call to repay your debt. If the value of the home drops, it has no impact as long as you make your monthly mortgage payment.

So, in real estate, because debt is stable, it can increase the ability to buy, which is a good thing.

LET'S UNDERSTAND HOW LEVERAGE WORKS FOR YOU.

Let's say you are a renter, and you inherit $100,000 and now have a decision to make. Should you buy stocks and bonds or precious metals, put them in a savings account, or purchase real estate?

Investment of $100,000 at 5%

NO LEVERAGE

Savings account $100,000 x 5% = $5,000

Stocks $100,000 x 5% yearly return = $5,000

Gold and silver at $100,000 x 5% yearly return = $5,000

WITH LEVERAGE

Real estate ($100,000 down and $400,000 debt)

$500,000 x 5% = $25 ,000

The earlier investment (that is, the $100,000 earning $5,000) had no leverage, whereas with the real estate, you use the $100,000 as your downpayment and get loaned $400,0000. Thus, you have leverage (of 4 times, or 400%) through a $400,000 mortgage debt for a total value of $500,000. Appreciation is based on the total value of the asset (including debt, not just the equity).

So, the $100,000 invested, combined with the $400,000 borrowed through the first mortgage, earned $25,000 or a 25% return on the investment of $100,000 with only a 5% increase in the value. It's no wonder why using debt to create leverage is one of the main advantages of owning real estate.

If you purchased the same $500,000 property with a $50,000 down payment and a $450,000 or 90% first mortgage, you would still get an appreciation of $25,000. Still, it is now a 50% return on the $50,000 invested as a down payment on a home. You would then have the other half of the original $100,000 to spend or invest.

People talk about real estate not being liquid, but the alternative of renting a home is also not liquid. With renting, you have no value being created and you have to either pay rent or get evicted.

Real estate is about having a place to live, and if you can make money or create wealth at the same time, then that is great.

That is why real estate is such a good investment. You need a place to live; you need shelter. Why not own a home and have it create value while also fulfilling your need for housing?

Remember, leverage is the process that adds value by increasing the ability to buy sooner using a mortgage and at a price higher than the available cash you have. You only need to save on the down payment and closing costs.

You can buy today using 100% financing. Other programs offer 3% to 5% down payments. The use of debt as leverage is much easier today. All you need is good credit and job stability.

I mention that leverage to help buyers realize mortgage debt has many advantages for them as buyers.

Consumer and car debt are to be avoided if possible or kept to a minimum since, as a rule, this type of debt, (unlike real estate debt) does not purchase assets that create or hold value. Instead, it goes into consumption, which is an expense—not a wealth creator.

POSTSCRIPT: TWO TRUE STORIES

Buying a home is a gold mine of opportunity, but there are also risks that buyers make mistakes about.

I have two true stories to share along the same lines about first-time buyers and two common mistakes that can be made.

I had a client who purchased one of my affordable housing projects. I sell units below market at cost plus a small profit. Remember, I am selling below market, so each buyer has free or built-in equity when they buy.

They qualified for a unit that was, say, 30% below market. They purchased it with a small down payment.

A few years later, the market collapsed, and owners nationwide went bankrupt to wipe out their debt. For many of these mainland foreclosures, it was needed because they were speculating and buying numerous properties for immediate resale, but there was no long-term plan or strategy to rent or resale. They were gambling with real estate. Speculation is not investing; greed is not investing. These people all lost because they looked at money instead of a realistic plan.

But back to my example...

The result of this was many stories in the news about tens of thousands of people being foreclosed on.

My client became concerned because their debt exceeded the unit's market value. In their minds, their investment in a home was underwater. They saw an attorney advertise to help people with homes that were underwater, meaning debt was greater than the value.

They declared bankruptcy, walked away from the unit, and rented an apartment in the same building.

Their rent was $900 a month. They were paying $800 a month to buy, but their debt was larger than the unit's value. The unfortunate part is that an attorney convinced them they had negative equity and should have declared bankruptcy, walked away through the foreclosure, and rented an apartment in the same building. The equity should not have mattered; the monthly payment was the reason for keeping the unit. The attorney did not understand real estate value and that the constant monthly payment saves the owner money particularly over time.

So, when the market recovered, their $100,000 unit grew to $300,000 in value. Unfortunately, they were renting next door and had paid $900 for rent instead of $800 to own a home. They were making their mortgage payment. They could have kept their unit but instead got bad advice and had to start all over.

They did not understand that a mortgage balance and the home's value do not matter as long as you can make the payment. It is your home.

Real estate is your home first and a wealth creator second.

Another couple was able to struggle to buy a new home. Nothing would stop them now. They were able to buy a home; the payment was affordable.

They could afford it, so they also purchased a new car.

Then they purchased some furniture, etc.

Their installment debt got too high, and they struggled.

Then, there was an economic slowdown, and work hours were cut.

They had no choice but to file for bankruptcy.

Their mistake was that they overreached for the more expensive new home, new cars, new this, new that.

It is IMPORTANT to think through your strategy. For other options, the prior example had been to: a) buy the home but live with what you have, do not buy a new car, furniture, etc.; or b) get a lower loan for a less expensive home and use the stepping stone technique where the dream home will still come, just a few years later. Then, you may be able to buy a car and furniture rather than make do with what you have.

Remember, we all have different needs and wants. If you need a new car, put that in your home-buying plan. If you are someone who wants nice furniture because it is important to you, put that into your buying decision.

It is not just about not buying any home; you need to be honest and determine which sacrifices you can make for a few years in order to start building generational wealth for your family.

Just keep in mind that the house is the foundation. The car and the furniture also need a home. Ownership is more important than renting or owning a car or new furniture.

WHAT WE HAVE LEARNED IN CHAPTER 9

1. Leverage is the fourth creator of wealth.

2. Leverage is the concept of using borrowed funds to increase your rate of return.

3. In real estate, leverage is created by a mortgage.

4. Real estate mortgages are long-term leverage and offer greater leverage than stocks, bonds, and precious metals investment options, along with negative equity protections not available to other investment options (such as margin calls).

5. A 5% return on $100,000 is $5,000 per year.

6. If the $100,000 is 20% down on a $500,000 property, the increase in value due to leverage goes from $5,000 to $25,000.

7. Leverage allows you to buy a more valuable asset by being able to borrow money.

8. Selling real estate can be a taxable event. This book is not about all aspects of real estate, but rather about how real estate creates wealth.

9. Real estate is not liquid, but neither is the alternative of renting. If you don't pay rent, you must move out.

10. The value created by leverage is accounted for in appreciation.

11. If you own or rent real estate, don't worry about value; worry about the monthly payment. Values can go up and down over time. Only be concerned that you are making a reasonable, affordable monthly payment.

12. You should realize that the payment to buy has all kinds of creators of wealth, so the cost to purchase is less than you think, and that renting gets no benefits, so rent is higher than what you pay.

13. Once you buy, don't splurge on new cars, furniture, etc. Be conservative; let time improve your position. Help the wealth creators create value for you.

14. Credit card debt can destroy the best-laid plans for creating wealth.

15. Looking at buying what you can afford and sacrificing now will bring big dividends in the future.

CHAPTER 10

THE FIFTH WEALTH CREATOR: THE SAVINGS ACCOUNT CALLED "MORTGAGE"

We identify the fifth wealth creator to be the savings account called "mortgage." In our example, we have a mortgage balance of $188,800. We've already talked about how the debt allows us to buy a property sooner since we don't have to save cash to buy. Trying to save some money would take so long that the price would go up faster than we could save. So, using leverage puts us on the road to ownership faster.

By qualifying for the new first mortgage, agreeing to take on the debt, and signing a note and mortgage to repay it, we have committed to saving that amount of money borrowed over the term of the loan—usually 15 to 30 years.

The buyers should see the mortgage as a forced savings account by making a monthly payment.

When you buy a home, you agree to make a monthly payment of principal and interest. The monthly principal reduces the debt until the loan is paid in full.

So, don't be afraid of debt; instead, look at it as a forced savings account. Suppose your mortgage is $188,800 or $400,000; whatever the mortgage balance is, there is an opportunity to save by making a monthly mortgage payment.

Make that payment every month knowing you are creating value for your family and your family's future.

You will be surprised at how a mortgage creates wealth for you and your family.

It has always amazed me how people are intimidated by mortgage debt. It is not their fault; it is the fault of our educational system, which has failed to teach students at any level the importance of real estate for the creation of wealth.

Everyone is involved with real estate. We live, work, play, and have fun in it. Real estate touches all our lives. We have to learn about real estate on our own.

So, let's look at our concern or fear of debt. We often use our fear or lack of knowledge about debt as the reason for not buying. It is the greatest indicator that we don't understand mortgage debt or home ownership.

We have all heard about or had a friend or family member who was foreclosed on. You see or hear about the unhappiness that follows.

However, it is more likely that you will be evicted from a rental unit than foreclosed on a home you own. The point is that regardless of renting or purchasing, you must pay the monthly rent or make a mortgage payment.

If you buy a home the "smart" way, keep payments affordable, and have reserves and a plan, you should never have to deal with foreclosure.

Understanding the wealth creators also gives you a chance to pay debt faster and save interest.

Look at purchasing a property that you like and can afford, but if you have an emergency—such as loss of your job or an illness—you should be prepared and have a plan.

No matter what you do in life, there are risks.

You need to understand that risk and be able to mitigate it.

In the worst case, if you get into trouble, you could sell the house and get or recover whatever you can from your investment and then prepare to buy again when you're ready.

Also, if a property is sold at a foreclosure sale, any funds left after paying the mortgage and cost are returned to the original owner.

If you run into a tough patch and have trouble with the payment, you could also rent the house out and let the tenant pay a rent that is high enough to cover the mortgage; you could then live with family or find a rental unit you can afford until you recover and can afford to move back into your home.

I guarantee that when you finish all the chapters in this book and understand the many advantages of a mortgage, you will know more about mortgages and how to create value than most owners and lenders in real estate today.

A mortgage is involved in almost every real estate purchase—especially for first-time buyers. The reality is that you cannot save money fast enough to pay cash for a property. Home prices will go up faster than you can save, and you also have to pay rent while saving. So, you borrow from a bank using a mortgage and agree to pay the debt over time. What would have been wasted on rent now goes toward ownership and creating value.

We learned about leverage in Chapter 9, as well as about the advantage of debt through leverage. It allows us to buy and start homeownership sooner. Leverage through a mortgage increases our rate of return on the investment in an owner-occupied home. Leverage also accelerates the creation of wealth.

But that is just one of many advantages to a mortgage. It is best to buy the best home as soon as possible rather than try and save money to buy your dream or perfect home.

Buying sooner with a mortgage debt allows you to put the wealth creators to work and create value sooner. Trying to save enough money to buy the perfect home is risky. Remember, we just learned that prices are increasing faster than you can save. You can't save fast enough to keep up with inflation.

In the future, when the time is right, you can sell or finance the present property and buy another home.

This is the steppingstone approach.

You take the first step by buying the best home or apartment you can afford at that time. Let real estate wealth creators create the value to take the second and third steps until you can buy your dream home.

Remember, at each step, you can sell the property and buy another or refinance it and buy another, keeping the first as a rental investment. If you refinance to buy a second property and keep the first property, you will then rent one out and live in the other. With this option, you have two properties that create value for you.

Most buyers are concerned about mortgages and feel pressured to make the payments and repay the lender. They see a mortgage as a necessary evil. They know the risk and are committed to making payments.

In reality, you have the same pressures when renting. You have to pay rent; you have to pay your landlord's mortgage. You have all the risk and responsibility in a different form, but you get none of the benefits.

A mortgage is your best friend. To understand the mortgage is to love the mortgage. Most buyers and owners don't consider a mortgage an advantage or wealth creator. You need to see and understand the mortgage as a wealth creator.

However, there are also other wealth creators buried in the mortgage process, which we will discuss in the next chapter.

The value of the savings account called the "mortgage" is the beginning mortgage balance. So, in this example, we can add $188,800 to our wealth creation through real estate ownership.

WHAT WE HAVE LEARNED IN CHAPTER 10

1. A mortgage is a written commitment to saving the amount of money borrowed over an agreed-upon time by agreeing to make monthly payments of principal and interest.

2. *Mortgage debt is good debt*. You are buying a place to live. The alternative is renting, where you buy a home for someone else. *Charge card debt is bad debt*.

3. You are buying real estate that will increase in value over time.

4. Real estate is part of everyone's life. We live in it, we work in it, and we shop in it—everything we do is tied to real estate. We do everything in (or on) real estate.

5. Our educational system has failed to teach us about real estate and the important role it plays in our lives.

6. Real estate creates wealth, better lives, and more opportunities.

7. Like everything in life, real estate has risks. By understanding real estate, however, you can control the risks.

8. If a crisis develops and you are forced into bankruptcy, it is not the end of the world. Figure out what went wrong and start over.

9. If a home is foreclosed and funds are left after paying all expenses, the funds go to you as the owner prior to foreclosure.

10. If you have a problem with payments, consider renting the home out while you live with family or rent an affordable unit.

11. Debt allows you to buy sooner and put the wealth creators to work for you. If you try and save for the purchase price, the values go up faster than you can save.

12. Using the steppingstone approach, you can buy the best you can afford, then a few years later, refinance and buy a second home, renting out the first. You now have two properties creating wealth. Or, you can sell and buy a new home and then repeat the process to get the home of your dreams.

13. The mortgage and mortgage debt are your best friends. To understand the mortgage is to love the mortgage.

CHAPTER 11

THE SIXTH WEALTH CREATOR: THE CONSTANT MONTHLY PAYMENT

I n our first chapter, we saw the difference between renting and buying. We looked at paying rent for a lifetime compared to the cost of purchasing a home with a 30-year mortgage. Our measuring stick was the total cost of both.

It's no question that renting costs more. When you rent, as your income goes up, the cost of rent goes up as well. When you buy a home or apartment, one advantage is getting a 30-year fixed rate loan with a constant monthly payment that stays the same for 30 years. This constant monthly payment is the sixth creator of wealth and is represented in our example by the principal and interest payment. Remember, the constant monthly mortgage payment reduces the cost of living by locking in your cost of housing for 30 years.

So, if you are a homeowner, your monthly payment will stay the same for 30 years. You get to keep that part of your income created by increases in your monthly pay over time.

If you rented, those pay raises would have gone to pay rent increases. Over the course of 30 years, it would be possible for your income to double or triple—and if you were renting, your rent could also double or triple.

Imagine: all those rent increases are yours if you are a homeowner and your landlord's if you rent.

The homeowner could use those increases in income to reduce the mortgage debt faster and pay off the loan sooner, saving thousands in interest and laying a solid foundation for buying investment properties and accelerating the creation of wealth.

Remember, future income savings are made possible by the constant monthly payment available in mortgage loans. The pay raises you would've spent on increasing rents can instead be spent on your style of living, investing in creating wealth, paying debt, sending your children to college, opening a business, and more. The critical point is that the constant monthly payment has made your life and your family not only better, but also happier and easier.

Insurance, water, electricity, gas, and food prices will rise over time. Your biggest monthly cost is your rent or your mortgage. If you buy a home, you can lock in your monthly payment for the term of the loan, and then when the mortgage is paid off you will have no payments.

I always recommend a 30-year fixed-rate loan, but other options exist. Some lenders may offer an adjustable-rate loan where the monthly payment and interest rate can fluctuate depending on the market.

To encourage you to take these loans, they may offer slightly lower interest rates to accept them.

The bank is making such loans because they believe interest rates will increase in the future, so they don't want to make a long-term commitment at a lower fixed rate.

If you are a homeowner and put the wealth creator of paying extra principal payments to work for you, then the adjustable-rate loan may not be the best choice.

Even though the 30-year loan may have a higher rate if you are making additional principal payments, by reducing your debt even faster, this will improve your position and increase your interest saved.

In an earlier chapter, we talked about taking advantage of the creators of wealth and using them to make even more money or use a portion of it to pay down debt.

At some point, if you and your family wanted to, you could buy another property using the funds saved by the constant monthly payment and put your knowledge of the wealth creators to work and buy investment properties.

Also, after 30 years, the constant monthly payment stops, and the loan is paid off. For the next 40 years, no mortgage is paid, and those funds can instead be invested to create more opportunities for you and your family. So, just in the last 40 years, you would save $1,013.20 monthly—or, for 480 months, you would save $486,336. This represents the mortgage payments you do not have to make for 40 years because you purchased a home and paid off the debt. The actual money saved would be *considerably more* since I used the constant monthly payment, not including any increases or pay raises over 40 years. However, this goes much further since the paid mortgage savings are small compared to what the constant monthly payment has provided to you in additional opportunities.

So, what are the opportunities and other potential forms of value the constant monthly payment wealth creator can bring to you and your family?

Well, for me, this is the greatest creator of wealth because it starts you into home ownership and creates less cost, which means more cash is available for you to invest in your lifestyle and other investments, such as real estate, stocks, bonds, precious metals, collectibles, fine art—you name it.

If a family decided to use the excess income that would have been rent to pay off debt on their home or buy another property, it would be very easy for them to create 10 million or more in equity by buying investments in real estate or stocks and bonds. All the wealth creators will work to create value.

This is how fortunes are made, and if you like and understand real estate, it is easy to create substantial wealth over many years simply by paying your mortgage and understanding the wealth creators that exist in real estate.

Buy one, two, or three properties, then start the process again and let the wealth creators do their jobs.

WHAT WE HAVE LEARNED IN CHAPTER 11

1. The sixth wealth creator is the constant monthly payment.

2. You lock in your housing cost for 30 years by buying a home.

3. Once you've paid off the mortgage, you have no mortgage payment to make.

4. Over the 30-year term of your mortgage, your employment income could easily double, triple, or quadruple.

5. In our earlier example, our family had an income of $900 a month in 1960. By 1990, their monthly income would have been between $5,000 and $7,000. By 2020, the family's income could be $10,000 to $20,000 per month.

6. History tells us that income increases over time can *add up*. Remember, you have to look at real estate and ownership and the wealth it creates over time.

7. By locking in your largest monthly expense housing cost as your income goes up, you can: 1) save pay raises; 2) invest pay raises; 3) pay down debt; and 4) have a better style of living.

8. If you do the first three, you will be able to pay off debt, buy stock, buy another property, etc.

9. The potential is more tremendous than you think. You can start buying investment properties that will result in more than your home; they will also create wealth.

10. This wealth creator has the potential to create millions in wealth depending on how you manage the process and put it to work.

11. To me, this is the greatest creator of wealth, and over a lifetime, can create millions in value—and easily ten million or more.

12. Remember, your mortgage payment is extra money once the loan is paid off.

13. Again, you need to thank and love your good friend, mortgage debt.

CHAPTER 12

THE SEVENTH WEALTH CREATOR: TAX SAVINGS

L et's discuss the seventh creator of wealth. The interest we pay to the lender on our home loan is tax-deductible. Interest paid on your mortgage loan is also tax-deductible, as is property tax paid to county governments and mortgage insurance. The IRS has determined that mortgage insurance, when it protects the lender and not you as a borrower (which is considered interest expense), is tax-deductible.

In our example of a $188,800 loan at 5%, the deductible items for interest total $859 for the first month.

We will use a tax due of 15%, 28%, or 31% for this calculation.

Depending on your tax bracket, you will have a monthly tax savings of $129, $241, or $266.

You don't pay taxes on the income used to pay interest. We can determine how much we save in taxes by multiplying the interest paid by our income tax rate. If renting, you pay no interest, so you have no deduction and pay higher taxes.

So, in our example, you save $241 per month in taxes using the middle amount.

You are also making a mortgage payment with a portion going to the debt reduction or the savings account called mortgage. So, you are benefiting from another $227 monthly by paying the principal down on the loan.

Your total savings compared to renting are $468 per month.

If you rent, you pay rent that covers or pays the landlord's mortgage—both principal and interest. In this example, you pay the interest, which is a tax deduction to the owner, saving him $241. Your rents pay the owner's mortgage, so you also pay the monthly principal on the owner's loan (savings account called "mortgage"). Remember, the principal pays down the loan, which can be recovered when the property is sold. The owner/landlord gets the full benefit of the $227 payment made to the principal. You get no benefit from paying rent but lose the monthly tax savings and principal.

You are paying your rent but also losing the benefits real estate creates. So, renting costs you an additional $468 in benefits/potential value each month.

If you pay rent twice (once to the landlord and then to Uncle Sam), you will get higher taxes and a loss of the principal payment. Basically, you have given it away to the landlord since you rent.

TENANT PAYS RENT TWICE

To put it another way, the renter struggles to pay the rent but pays rent twice—once to the landlord and a second time in the form of higher taxes.

So, a tenant who rents for $1,200 also pays Uncle Sam another $241 in taxes. The rent allows the landlord to pay his mortgage and build equity of $227 in principal. So, the total loss to the tenant is not $241 in tax savings. The tenant loses another $227 in principal paid on the mortgage, for a total monthly cost of $468 (taxes and principal).

So, if you rent for $1,200, you can buy for $1,441 (tax savings) to $1,688 (tax savings and principal) without it being a greater burden than your rent.

Instead of paying Uncle Sam taxes every month, you can use the funds to buy a home. If you count the principal as your savings account, you can pay even more monthly and not have a greater burden than the rent.

So, rent of $1,200 really costs $1,688.

We added the principal to the cost of renting when comparing renting to owning since the tenant pays the rent monthly, and the rent includes the seller's mortgage payment. The landlord gets all the benefits as the owner, and the tenant receives none.

There are other tax benefits, but I will not cover them because this book is not about taxes, but rather about the wealth creators in real estate.

Your accountant or realtor should be able to answer or refer you to an expert who can answer tax questions.

Remember that while the wealth creators generate a great deal of potential wealth, other tax benefits are available to owners and not renters.

The tax issues are complex and could be a separate book.

I will mention the most frequently used ones. These are not in our discussion comparing renting to buying since we are looking at a monthly comparison of renting to owning.

It's good to know the taxes are out there. Taxes can change as the law changes, and I only mention them to show the potential and value of real estate, along with how complex it can be.

The present book attempts to provide some basic knowledge of real estate and show why you should buy and not rent. This is the beginner's or freshman's class.

Many other books will go into more detail—including the sophomore, junior, and senior classes. For now, we shall return to Class 101.

BACK TO TAXES

The first additional tax benefit is paying points and/or finance fees when you buy a home. It is basically prepaid interest. These numbers appear on your bank closing statement and are tax-deductible.

For all tax income refunds you receive from the State of Hawaii and the federal government, at least 50% of all tax refunds you may pay in as principal and have it go to debt reduction as a principal prepayment.

The mortgage interest credit is a tax benefit the state and federal government give. It is for low-income buyers and includes more people than you think.

Let's unpack this further: the federal mortgage interest credit and the State of Hawaii's. Do not forget to contact your local tax advisor to see what may be available in your county, state, and locality. Let's continue...

The federal government provides a federal mortgage interest credit (MCC). This allows you, the homeowner, to claim a percentage of the mortgage interest paid each year as a direct reduction of your federal tax liability. Unlike mortgage interest deduction (which reduces taxable income), the mortgage interest credit reduces the amount of tax you owe dollar for dollar. This means it may be more beneficial than a deduction in some cases because it directly lowers your tax bill.

Further, some states have mortgage interest credits that directly improve your monthly cash flow, such as the one we operate in—the State of Hawaii. The State of Hawaii provides a Hawaii mortgage interest credit (HMIC) in that if you meet the qualifications, instead of taking a lump sum tax refund or deduction at the end of the year, the State of Hawaii permits a credit to be applied directly to your monthly mortgage payment, improving your cash flow and budgeting. This allows buyers to reduce their payments by using the tax refund monthly rather than at the end of the year. If available in your state or locality, this is a great program that takes the payment down monthly by crediting your end-of-year tax refund each month to reduce your cash outflow.

I had a client earning $70,000 who qualified for the mortgage interest credit and received a mortgage credit certificate that reduced her monthly tax deduction from her pay, so she got her tax refund monthly to help pay her mortgage. She did not have to wait till the end of the year. If I remember correctly, she got a credit of over $300 per month to help with the payment.

As you can see, the tax issues really become a book unto themselves. (*Fun fact:* tax code is over 20,000 pages long.)

Here is a quick overview of what to ask your tax advisor for. Both federal and state county programs can be taken advantage of.

Here is a recap and list of a simple web search of available programs and associated definitions:

Federal Tax Savings Programs

1. Mortgage Interest Deduction:
   - What it is: You can deduct the interest you pay on your mortgage loan (up to a limit) from your taxable income.
   - How it helps: Reduces your taxable income, which lowers the amount of tax you owe.
   - Eligibility: Available for mortgage loans on your primary residence and second homes (up to a $750,000 loan limit for new mortgages, or $1 million if the loan was taken before December 15, 2017).

2. Mortgage Insurance Premiums Deduction:

   o What it is: If you pay private mortgage insurance (PMI) or FHA mortgage insurance, you may be able to deduct those premiums from your taxable income.

   o How it helps: Reduces your taxable income.

   o Eligibility: Available for primary and second homes. The deduction phases out at higher income levels.

3. Capital Gains Exclusion on Sale of Home:

   o What it is: If you sell your primary home and meet specific requirements, you can exclude up to $250,000 of the gain ($500,000 for married couples) from taxes.

   o How it helps: Excludes the profit from the sale of your home from taxable income.

   o Eligibility: You must have owned and lived in the home for at least two out of the last five years before the sale.

4. Home Office Deduction (for self-employed homeowners):

   o What it is: If you use part of your home regularly and ex-clusively for business, you may be able to deduct certain home office expenses.

   o How it helps: Reduces taxable income by deducting a por-tion of your home-related expenses.

   o Eligibility: The space must be used for business purposes and meet specific IRS requirements.

5. Energy Efficiency Tax Credits:

   o What it is: The IRS offers tax credits for making energy-ef-ficient improvements to your home, like installing solar panels or energy-efficient windows.

- How it helps: Reduces your tax liability through direct credits.
- Eligibility: Available for specific energy-efficient home up-grades. For example, 30% of the cost of installing solar energy systems is credited back (up to certain limits).

6. First-Time Homebuyer Tax Credit (for specific cases):

- What it is: There was previously a tax credit for first-time homebuyers, but it has been phased out. However, you may qualify for other programs through your state or local government.
- How it helps: This program helped first-time buyers with down payments or closing costs.

7. Standard Deduction:

- What it is: Homeowners can claim the standard deduction, which reduces their taxable income. The amount is higher for married couples filing jointly and single filers over 65.
- How it helps: Reduces your taxable income by the set deduction amount, which may lower your tax bill.

8. State and Local Property Tax Deduction:

- What it is: You can deduct up to $10,000 ($5,000 if married filing separately) in state and local property taxes, as well as other state and local taxes like income or sales taxes, combined.
- How it helps: Reduces taxable income by allowing deductions on property and state/local taxes.

9. Mortgage Credit Certificate (MCC) (for first-time buyers in some states):

   o What it is: This is a federal program offered by state or local governments that provides a tax credit for a portion of your mortgage interest payments.

   o How it helps: Directly reduces your tax bill (as opposed to a deduction).

State-Level Tax Savings Programs for Homeowners:

(Note: State programs vary widely, so you should check your state's specific offerings. Below are examples of common programs available in many states.)

1. State-Specific Mortgage Interest Deductions:

   o What it is: Some states offer their own mortgage interest deduction, allowing you to deduct a portion of your mortgage interest from state income taxes.

   o How it helps: Lowers your state taxable income.

2. Property Tax Relief Programs:

   o What it is: Many states offer property tax relief or exemptions for certain homeowners, such as senior citizens, veterans, or low-income homeowners.

   o How it helps: Reduces the amount of property taxes you need to pay, either through exemptions or credits.

   o Eligibility: Often based on age, income, or disability status.

3. State-Based First-Time Homebuyer Programs:

    o   What it is: States may offer tax credits or down payment assistance for first-time homebuyers to help with closing costs or down payments.

    o   How it helps: Lowers the upfront costs of purchasing a home.

    o   Eligibility: Generally available to first-time buyers and sometimes to those purchasing in specific areas.

4. Home Energy Efficiency Credits or Rebates:

    o   What it is: Some states offer credits or rebates for energy-efficient home improvements, like installing insulation, solar panels, or energy-efficient appliances.

    o   How it helps: Reduces the cost of energy-saving upgrades and lowers your state tax bill.

5. Homestead Exemption:

    o   What it is: Many states offer a homestead exemption which reduces the taxable value of your property, lowering the amount of property tax you owe.

    o   How it helps: Lowers your property tax bill by exempting a portion of your home's value from taxation.

    o   Eligibility: Often available for primary residences, and eligibility may depend on income, age, or disability status.

6. State-Specific Property Tax Circuit Breaker Programs:

    o   What it is: These programs are designed to provide tax relief to low-income or senior homeowners by "capping" the amount of property taxes they must pay relative to their income.

- How it helps: Reduces your property taxes based on income or age.

- Eligibility: Typically, available to low-income or senior homeowners.

7. State-Specific Tax Credits for Homeowners:

- What it is: Some states offer specific tax credits for homeowners, such as credits for renovation work, home repairs, or improvements to preserve historic homes.

- How it helps: Directly reduces the amount of taxes you owe.

- Eligibility: Varies based on location and specific types of renovations or repairs.

8. State and Local Energy Efficiency Loan or Incentive Programs:

- What it is: Many states and local governments offer low-interest loans or grants for home energy improvements, like upgrading insulation or installing solar panels.

- How it helps: Reduces the cost of making energy-efficient improvements and may come with tax credits or deductions.

- Eligibility: Depends on your location and the type of energy improvement you are looking for.

BACK TO THE RENT OR OWN COMPARISON

When comparing renting to owning, the important point is that a tenant pays more than the base rent amount but does not realize it. The tenant can afford to pay more monthly to buy since he is already paying rent and the other hidden costs anyway.

We are using this point to encourage renters to use the knowledge of the wealth creators to look at buying and start creative wealth for themselves, not the landlord.

WHAT WE HAVE LEARNED IN CHAPTER 12

1. Real estate has a number of tax advantages; in this book, we only covered a few of them. These wealth creators can be found on the rent vs. buy worksheet.

2. Your realtor or tax advisor can explain other tax advantages in real estate (as shown in our recap of what can be found on a simple web search).

3. The tax-deductible items are interest, property taxes, and mortgage insurance for lenders (not life insurance for borrowers, which is not tax-deductible).

4. A renter pays rent monthly but also pays rent a second time to Uncle Sam in the form of higher taxes. So, if you rent, you spend hundreds more in taxes.

5. We are comparing rent to owning, but I am going to mention additional tax advantages you should be aware of, such as finance fees and points paid at the closing of the mortgage being tax-deductible.

6. There is a mortgage interest credit that is issued by states and the federal government which helps you qualify for a loan by issuing a mortgage credit certificate. This can be 10% to 15% of mortgage interest.

7. When selling, you also qualify for a capital gain exclusion of $250,000 if single and $500,000 if married. This means that money is tax-free, although there are also occupancy requirements, etc., so talk to your realtor and tax advisor.

8. If you are renovating and upgrading windows, doors, etc., see if it qualifies for an energy tax credit.

9. If upgrading for medical, you may not qualify for additional tax credits.

10. The tax concept of basis should be discussed based on the purchase price. If you upgrade or add rooms, you can add qualified

upgrades. If a portion of the home is destroyed (say, the garage burns down), you subtract that value from the basis, but you can add the cost of the new garage.

11. The basis is important because it will be used to determine the taxable portion of the sale.

12. If you want to learn more about these tax issues, the IRS has good pamphlets available that explain them as well.

13. **IMPORTANT:** Ask your realtor and tax expert to help with tax issues and which programs may be available to improve your cash flow, reduce your tax basis, etc. This information is invaluable when used in conjunction with the worksheets provided to determine the cost of renting vs. owning and planning your journey.

CHAPTER 13

THE EIGHTH WEALTH CREATOR: MORTGAGE'S SURPRISE BENEFIT – IT PAYS YOU PRINCIPAL

The mortgage pays you a return in the form of "interest that becomes principal," and this is better than a savings account. Again, the mortgage is full of surprises that create value for you as the property owner. The second-largest value created in the mortgage is the interest the mortgage pays to the borrower.

TOTAL PAYMENTS MADE

The total payments made over 30 years would be the monthly principal and interest payment times 30-year amortization. In the case of the $188,800 loan, we are using our example:

Monthly Mortgage Payment $1,013.52

X 360 Months (30 Years)

= $364,867 in (Total Payments)

So, the total payment made is $364,867.

How much of the total is principal, and how much is interest? We know what we borrowed, so we will subtract the loan amount of $188,800 from the total paid. The remaining balance is the amount that was paid as interest.

The math is:

Total Payments of $364,867 (Principal & Interest)

- $188,800 (Principal)

= $176,067 (Interest) Paid

LET'S BREAK DOWN THE MONTHLY PAYMENT OF PRINCIPAL AND INTEREST.

Our monthly mortgage payment of $1,013.52 is broken down into two parts: the principal would be $226.85, and the interest would be $786.67.

If the monthly payment allocation to principal and interest did not change, we would pay as principal.

$226.85 first month principal x 360 months = $81,666

If interest stayed the same as the first month's payment, it would be:

$786.67 x 360 months = $283,201

The combination of the two numbers represents the maximum that can be paid and a total of $364,867. We know the totals are correct since the total is the same in both cases. The total borrowed was $188,800, but the above calculation of the principal paid over 30 years comes out to $81,666, not the $188,800 we borrowed. We are short $107,134 on the principal paid.

As to the interest in our earlier calculation, we subtracted the loan of $188,800 being paid from the total of all payments made and we had interest paid of $176,067.

However, our recent calculation shows that based on the first month's interest payment, we could have paid $283,201 in interest, not the actual amount of $176,067. So, the allocation to principal and interest must have changed during the 30-year amortization of the loan.

The difference between the two interest amounts was $107,134, and we got that number by subtracting $176,067, and what we could have paid in interest of $283,201. We overpaid interest by $107,134.

When this number ($107,134) is added to the $81,666, what is the total principal paid?

We get a total of $188,800, which is the mortgage amount that was paid off.

SO, WHAT HAPPENED?

All this math has shown is that $107,134 of interest was paid over 30 years on the portion of the loan going to the principal. The interest that would have been paid on the principal was credited monthly to the loan and, in the process, converted to principal. We spent only $81,666 in principal through our monthly payment. The difference is due to $107,134 of interest being paid as interest on the principal paid and automatically converting to principal, so there is no tax on interest earned.

In the first month, our payment of $1,013.52 was $786.67 in interest and $226.85 in principal. The following month, the interest will be computed again on a lower mortgage balance since we made a principal payment of $226.85. This means the payment remains the same, but the allocation to principal and interest will change monthly. Interest goes down, and the principal goes up each month until the loan is fully paid. So, the interest due for the second month will be less because $226.85 has been paid down on principal the previous month. The mortgage balance is lower by that amount.

In view of the above, the second month's interest is calculated on the smaller loan balance ($188,800 - first month's principal $226.85 = new mortgage balance for second month $188,573.15. The interest saved and credited to the principal is the same interest that would have been paid on the portion of the loan paid off. That principal calculation for the mortgage balance after the first payment to the principal comes is now $188,573.15 (i.e., $ 188,800 - $226.85 =$188,573).

Since the payment can only be allocated to principal or interest, that extra interest in the second month becomes principal and is applied to reduce the debt.

SO, HOW DOES THE LOAN PAY YOU $107,134 IN INTEREST?

We will look at the amortization schedule shortly to show you where all this magic occurred. But let's first make sure we get the numbers and the concept.

In our example, all the numbers are known before we start. The beginning mortgage balance is $188,800—the monthly payments of $1,013.52.

We did the math to break out the first month's payment into two parts: principal of $226.85 and interest of $786.67.

The only thing that will change in the amortization process is the allocation to principal and interest, and the mortgage balance declines as the principal is credited after each payment.

For the second month, the math shows that the mortgage balance owed is $188,573.

The monthly total payment remains the same, but the allocation to principal and interest changes each month. As the principal is paid down on the loan, interest is no longer paid on the portion that was used to pay the principal down. Interest is paid on the remaining or current balance owing, which declines monthly as the principal is paid on the loan. As the principal goes down, the next month's interest expense decreases. That reduction in interest expense has to go somewhere. There are only two choices: principal or interest. The question is, how did interest become principal?

The answer is that as interest on the principal is paid, it automatically becomes the principal.

So, monthly, we paid a total of $81,666 in principal, and the mortgage paid us 5% interest on the principal payments, making it a total interest earned of $107,134 on the loan. This was possible due to the process within the amortization schedule where interest that was being charged on the loan (a portion of which would have been interest on the amount paid down) converts from interest to principal.

We earned $107,134 in interest from the savings account called mortgage. You knew you had borrowed $188,800 and never realized that you only paid back $81,666. The balance of $107,134 was paid as interest but credited to the principal. Don't feel bad; very few people realize it.

God! I love my first mortgage, I love real estate, and I love creating wealth and value for my family.

And better yet, we earned the interest tax-free. The mortgage is the friend that never stops giving.

CHAPTER 14

THE MAGIC OF AMORTIZATION

Let's now look at how the amortization process works and creates a tax-free interest of $107,134 for us. To do that, we will highlight certain areas of our amortization table to walk through the key takeaways and mechanics of how the concepts we will unpack in this chapter work. (*Note: a fuller amortization table may be found at the end of the book as well. You can also find the full complete table on (www.savio.com/rentvsbuy or www.saviomanagement.com/rentvs-buy).

The amortization table example we use will be a loan of $188,800 at 5% interest amortized over 30 years.

The amortization table is just the printed record of your projected monthly principal and interest payments. Every loan will have a different schedule unless all terms are the same. Those terms are the loan amount, the interest rate, and the original term of the loan. You can see how if the mortgage balance, term, interest, or amortization changes, it would affect an ingredient in the amortization schedule and create the need for a unique schedule for the loan being reviewed.

Before we begin, as a present or potential owner of real estate, you should have a good understanding of mortgages and how they create value for you, as well as some misunderstandings about them, one of which is interest. Think of the interest rate as the *alleged* cost to *"rent"* purchase power (even though, as we will discover, there is more to the story).

Note that you may use a variety of free amortization calculators available on the internet to help with these calculations.

We will show two amortization schedules: the first is an example of the typical amortization schedule for a real estate loan (Columns 1 through 5), with the additional columns hidden; and the second will reveal that these columns have more detail, so you can be sure to understand how interest is earned as a tax-free principal.

Let's begin by highlighting portions of the amortization schedule to better illustrate the relevant points. As shown below in the amortization schedule, you can see in the columns how the principal and interest are credited each month. The titles at the top will help identify which column we are talking about. So, let's go through each column first. I have numbered them "1" through "5" for easy reference.

Column 1	Column 2	Column 3	Column 4	Column 5	Column 6	Column 7
Event	Payment	Interest	Principal	Balance	Interest to Principal	Cumulative

Column 1, "Event," is the monthly payment number or event. If a loan is a 30-year term and requires a monthly payment, it will have 360 payment events; likewise, if it is a 15-year loan, it will have 180 payment events. *Remember, our real estate loans usually have a fixed monthly payment that is constant during the term of the loan.*

Column 2, "Payment," is the constant monthly payment needed to fully amortize the loan over the agreed term.

Column 3, "Interest," is the month's interest charged on the remaining balance still owed or the balance of the loan still outstanding.

Column 4, "Principal," is the portion of the monthly payment that is principal and goes to pay down the loan.

Column 5, "Balance," is the first line on this page and all other pages and is the original balance of the loan. In our example, we are using a balance of $188,800; all calculations or balances after that are the mortgage balance. Once that month's principal payment has been credited to the loan, the new balance owed once a payment is made becomes the balance used to determine the interest charged for the following month. All balances after that are the mortgage balance after the monthly payment of the principal has been made. The new balance owed on the loan will be used to determine the next month's interest.

At this point, let's add the first event or payment to our column numbers and subject headers.

Column 1	Column 2	Column 3	Column 4	Column 5	Column 6	Column 7
Event	Payment	Interest	Principal	Balance	▇▇▇▇	▇▇
Loan 1				$188,800.00		
Payment 1	$1,013.52	$786.67	$226.85	$188,573.15		

Let's look at the first event or payment. The total payment was $1013.52, and that is shown in Column 2; Column 3 represents the interest of $786.67. The interest is calculated by taking our beginning balance of $188,800 and multiplying it by 5%, which gives us the interest for the year. Then, you divide that amount by 12 months to arrive at the first month's interest. That interest is next deducted from Column 2, which is your principal and interest payment of $1013.52. When the interest is subtracted from the columns to the monthly payment, we arrive at the amount of the principal payment: $226.85. That amount is deducted from the $188,800, which gives us our new mortgage balance of $188,573.15. This process will continue until the loan is paid, as demonstrated in some of the following tables.

NOW, LET'S LOOK AT LARGE CHANGES OVER A PERIOD OF TIME.

This chart shows payment and amortization over *time*. Before we go on with the monthly amortization schedule, let's stop and take a look at the chart below, which shows the payments during the first event, payments during the 180th event, and payments during the 360th event to give you an idea of how much the amortizations change over time.

Column 1	Column 2	Column 3	Column 4	Column 5	Column 6	Column 7
Event	Payment	Interest	Principal	Balance	▬	▬
Loan 1				$188,800.00		
Payment 1	$1,013.52	$786.67	$226.85	$188,573.15	▬	▬
Payment 180	$1,013.52	$536.01	$477.51	$128,164.64	▬	▬
Payment 360	$1,012.93	$4.20	$1,008.73	$0.00	▬	▬

The first thing you will notice is that Column 2 has not changed. The loan is a constant monthly payment, and every payment is $1013.52. When you look at Column 3, you see that the interest has changed. The first interest payment was $786.67, the 180th was $536.01, and the last was $4.20.

The principal started at $226.85. However, by the 180th month, with an interest payment of $536.01, the principal is up to $477.51, and the final 360th-month payment has an interest of $4.20 and a principal payment of $1,008.73.

This truly shows how interest earned on the principal payments increases due to interest being reduced every month since the balance of the loan is going down. Interest is always computed on the balance of the debt owed. As the debt is reduced and the interest amount owed goes down, that difference can only be credited to the *principal*.

Remember, there were only two parts to a fully amortized mortgage payment: principal and interest.

LET'S LOOK AT THE MONTHLY CHANGES THAT ARE ON THE AMORTIZATION SCHEDULE BUT NOT CLEARLY IDENTIFIED.

At this stage, we'll reveal the hidden columns, Column 6 and Column 7. Drumroll, please...

It may not be as exciting as a ride at an amusement park, but hopefully you find it as financially exciting as I do!

Column 6, "Interest to Principal," is the amount of interest that converts to the principal on that month's interest. To compute the amount of interest in this example, take Column 4 and multiply by the interest rate of 5%. That gives you a yearly savings of $11.35. Divide that by 12 months, and you will get $0.95 in principal from interest.

Column 7, "Cumulative," is the amount of interest being converted to principal cumulative from all prior months that are being added to the principal paid.

We have already discussed the first monthly payment, so now, using the following table, let's look at the payment as it progresses through the first five months.

Column 1	Column 2	Column 3	Column 4	Column 5	Column 6	Column 7
Event	Payment	Interest	Principal	Balance	Current Month Interest to Principal	Cumulative Total for the Previous Month(s) Interest to Principal
Loan 1				$188,800.00		

Payment 1	$1,013.52	$786.67	$226.85	$188,573.15		
Payment 2	$1,013.52	$785.72	$227.80	$188,345.35	$0.95	$0.95
Payment 3	$1,013.52	$784.77	$228.75	$188,116.60	$0.95	$1.90
Payment 4	$1,013.52	$783.82	$229.70	$187,886.90	$0.95	$2.85
Payment 5	$1,013.52	$782.86	$230.66	$187,656.24	$0.96	$3.81

To reiterate, we have uncovered the hidden columns to demonstrate the concept of interest on principal at *work!* Column 6 is Interest to Principal, and Column 7 is Cumulative. After the first payment, the process of converting interest to principal has started.

If you scroll down the Interest column (Column 3), you will notice that the interest is going down every single month. If you look at the Principal column (Column 4), you will see it is going up every month.

Remember that the interest on the principal paid has to go somewhere, so it is added to the following month's payment as a principal payment.

Column 6 accounts for the monthly *addition* representing the interest that would've been paid to the lender. Since the principal payment was made, the interest on that payment goes to the *owner* of the property. You will notice how it goes up very slowly every single month.

Column 7 is the cumulative total, representing the full payment for that month and all previous months. So, what does it look like over the term of the loan? Basically, we are saving $0.95 in the first month, but we are saving that for 359 months for a total of $341.05 over the life of the loan.

The second payment in month 2 also saves $0.95 for 358 months, or $340.10 over the life of the loan.

Now, if you look at Column 7, we show the cumulative amount paid every month, so the first month is $0.95, the second is $1.90, the third is $2.85, the fourth is $3.81, and it goes on and on for 30 years, growing a little bit each month and adding up to the cumulative that will result in our buyer earning $107,134.32 in interest during the term of this loan.

Let's reveal how we arrived at $107,134.32 in interest earned during the term of this loan.

We will now add two more columns: the *super-secret* Column 8 and Column 0. Column 8 will represent each month's interest converted to the principal (Column 4) times the remaining term of the loan. Column 0 will show the remaining months left on the loan. To provide further clarity as to how this quickly accumulates to ~$107,000 earned on the loan, let's revisit the table for the first five months.

Column 0	Column 1	Column 2	Column 3	Column 4	Column 5	Column 6	Column 7	Column 8
Months Remaining	Event	Payment	Interest	Principal	Balance	Current Month Interest to Principal	Cumulative Total for the Previous Month(s) Interest to Principal	Interest to Principal Earned on Remainder of Loan
	Loan 1				$188,800.00			
360	Payment 1	$1,013.52	$786.67	$226.85	$188,573.15			
359	Payment 2	$1,013.52	$785.72	$227.80	$188,345.35	$0.95	$0.95	$341.05
358	Payment 3	$1,013.52	$784.77	$228.75	$188,116.60	$0.95	$1.90	$340.10
357	Payment 4	$1,013.52	$783.82	$229.70	$187,886.90	$0.95	$2.85	$339.15
356	Payment 5	$1,013.52	$782.86	$230.66	$187,656.24	$0.96	$3.81	$341.76

This demonstrates how, for the first five months, $1,362.06 of interest has already been converted to principal or interest earned on the principal.

The $0.95 in Column 6 saved times the remainder of the loan term in Column 0 equals the interest converted to principal over the remainder of the loan in Column 8. Thus, just $0.95 that month over the remainder of the loan (which starts at $0.95 times 359 months remaining) converts $341.06 of interest to the principal.

When extrapolated out for 30 years, it totals $107,134.22, which is an average of $3571.13 interest to principal each year. This comes out to a 1.9% earned average for each of the 30 years of interest on the principal. It gets weirder when you calculate your true interest rate, in that for our example, the loan at 5% is actually 3.1%. Because of this, there is 1.9% interest earned on the principal.

As an IMPORTANT side takeaway, there is a key lesson here lurking in the math. Early additional principal payments have a big impact! If we had made a $10,000 principal payment in the first year, we would have saved $14,500 in interest. $10,000 x 5% = $500 per year x 29 years = $14,500. In short, prepayments save tremendous amounts of interest. Secondly, the earlier, the *better!*

If we pay $10,000 in the last year, we will only save $500 in interest since interest is only paid for one year.

Thus, remember prior to continuing to re-stress this takeaway on the lesson lurking in the math: if you make additional principal payments as soon as possible after you originate the loan, even if only a few dollars a month, it accelerates the interest savings. This is often possible—but remember, you have tax savings at the end of the year. Further, do not forget to THINK about taking portions of raises to further accelerate the paydown of the loan and increase your interest saved. You could adjust your lifestyle by giving up lunches or dinners out or Starbucks Coffee and then trying to save $20 a week to pay down your loan.

Let's continue to take a closer look at the amortization schedule because this leads into the real brain twister: the 5% mortgage is not truly

5%. It's less, and significantly so. And how is that, you may ask? Well, let's continue our journey...

See the amortization table for areas we will focus on in the following pages.

To reiterate, Column 6 (Interest to Principal) shows the difference between interest and principal each month, which converts to principal the following month.

This represents the difference in the interest charged from month to month. I didn't do this for the whole column, but just the first nine payments of the first year and the 180th and 360th months. While I am conducting redundancy in the appearance of the charts, it is to illustrate the point and prevent too much page-flipping.

Column 1	Column 2	Column 3	Column 4	Column 5	Column 6	Column 7
Event	Payment	Interest	Principal	Balance	Interest to Principal	Cumulative
Loan 1				$188,800.00		
Payment 1	$1,013.52	$786.67	$226.85	$188,573.15		
Payment 2	$1,013.52	$785.72	$227.80	$188,345.35	$0.95	$0.95
Payment 3	$1,013.52	$784.77	$228.75	$188,116.60	$0.95	$1.90
Payment 4	$1,013.52	$783.82	$229.70	$187,886.90	$0.95	$2.85
Payment 5	$1,013.52	$782.86	$230.66	$187,656.24	$0.96	$3.81
Payment 6	$1,013.52	$781.90	$231.62	$187,424.62	$0.96	$4.77
Payment 7	$1,013.52	$780.94	$232.58	$187,192.04	$0.96	$5.73
Payment 8	$1,013.52	$779.97	$233.55	$186,958.49	$0.97	$6.70
Payment 9	$1,013.52	$778.99	$234.53	$186,723.96	$0.98	$7.68

For the 180th month, the interest difference is $1.99 compared to the previous month.

Column 1	Column 2	Column 3	Column 4	Column 5	Column 6	Column 7
Event	Payment	Interest	Principal	Balance	Interest to Principal	Cumulative
Payment 179	$1,013.52	$537.99	$475.53	$128,642.15	$1.97	$248.68
Payment 180	$1,013.52	$536.01	$477.51	$128,164.64	$1.99	$250.66

The monthly difference in the payment has grown from $0.95 (the difference between the first- and second-month payments) to a $1.99 difference between the 179th payment and the 180th payment.

Remember that Column 6 is the interest earned on the principal payment for that month only. All other monthly or cumulative conversions of interest to the principal are now included in the present principal payments. It started at $0.95 per month and has grown to almost $2 per month. When added to the original principal payment of $226.85, the monthly savings of interest due to principal paydown are $0.95 to $1.99, which is why it has converted from $266.85 to $477.51 by month 180. Looking at Column 4 ("Principal") demonstrates this in action, showing the growth of principal from $226.85 to $477.50.

The schedule shows both the monthly difference and the total monthly difference for all payments, as well as how it will continue to grow a little each month till the loan is paid in full.

INCREASE IN PRINCIPAL IS THE REDUCTION IN INTEREST.

The reduction in interest is the difference in the amount of interest of what would have been paid if no payments to the principal had been made—and the lower the interest paid, on the lower balance after deducting a principal payment.

The amortization process converts the interest that would have been paid to the lender on that month's principal payment to interest on the principal paid, which becomes principal.

LET'S EXPLAIN THE PAYMENTS ANOTHER WAY.

Multiply present loan balance x by interest rate = one year's interest.

$188,800 x 5% = $9,440 due as interest. *But we need the monthly interest.*

So, we then divide interest for the year by 12 months = that monthly interest.

$9,440 divided by 12 months = $786.67 monthly interest. This agrees with the amortization schedule for the first month's interest, so it is correct.

Also, remember that our loan is paid monthly, so the balance changes monthly.

We then need to find the principal, so we take the:

Monthly mortgage payment - INTEREST = principal in monthly payment

$1,013.52 - $786.67 = $226.85

Again, we agree with the amortization schedule, so it is correct.

We then take the:

Mortgage balance - principal paid

So, $188,800 - $226.85 = $188,573.15, being the new balance.

Again, we agree with the amortization schedule.

SO, LET'S LOOK AT WHAT IS NOT SHOWN IN THE AMORTIZATION SCHEDULE

If you multiply the first principal payment of $226.85 by 5% interest, you will get $11.34, which is interest on that balance for the year. If you divide the yearly interest by 12 months, you get interest of $.0.95 for that month. That 95 cents is the monthly interest on the $226.85 principal paid for that month—and along with the principal, the interest is credited to reduce debt. This interest paid/earned on the $226.85 is 5%, which will continue to compound through the entire term of the loan. This is shown in Column 6, "Interest to Principal."

This information is shown on the printed amortization schedule, seen in the column "Interest to Principal." You will see I calculated it for nine months on the table (shown again below). It is the monthly interest saved, not the cumulative (which is Column 7).

Column 1	Column 2	Column 3	Column 4	Column 5	Column 6	Column 7
Event	Payment	Interest	Principal	Balance	Interest to Principal	Cumulative
Loan 1				$188,800.00		
Payment 1	$1,013.52	$786.67	$226.85	$188,573.15		
Payment 2	$1,013.52	$785.72	$227.80	$188,345.35	$0.95	$0.95
Payment 3	$1,013.52	$784.77	$228.75	$188,116.60	$0.95	$1.90
Payment 4	$1,013.52	$783.82	$229.70	$187,886.90	$0.95	$2.85
Payment 5	$1,013.52	$782.86	$230.66	$187,656.24	$0.96	$3.81
Payment 6	$1,013.52	$781.90	$231.62	$187,424.62	$0.96	$4.77
Payment 7	$1,013.52	$780.94	$232.58	$187,192.04	$0.96	$5.73
Payment 8	$1,013.52	$779.97	$233.55	$186,958.49	$0.97	$6.70
Payment 9	$1,013.52	$778.99	$234.53	$186,723.96	$0.98	$7.68

LET'S LOOK AT THE AMORTIZATION SCHEDULE AGAIN.

Now, for the 180th month—or halfway through the amortization schedule of 360 months (30 years).

Column 1	Column 2	Column 3	Column 4	Column 5	Column 6	Column 7
Event	Payment	Interest	Principal	Balance	Interest to Principal	Cumulative
Payment 179	$1,013.52	$537.99	$475.53	$128,642.15	$1.97	$248.68
Payment 180	$1,013.52	$536.01	$477.51	$128,164.64	$1.99	$250.66
Payment 360	$1,013.52	$4.21	$1,009.31	$0.00	$4.18	$782.46

This shows that in the first months, $0.95 added to the monthly savings grew to a total monthly interest earned of $250.66 converted to principal in the 180th month. The interest went from $786.67 in the first month to $536.01 in the 180th month. The principal went from $226.85 the first month to $477.51 in the 180th month, or halfway through the amortization. Interest went down by the exact amount of the increase in the principal because the principal is earning 5% interest and continues to compound, reducing the effective interest.

Remember Column 6: when you subtract the monthly mortgage balances from the beginning balance, you determine the cumulative total paid to reduce the principal.

In the 360th month of the final payment, we see the interest that started at $786.67 has declined to where the interest expense is now only $4.20 for the last month. The interest converted to principal is $782.47 for that previous month.

The principal started at $226.85, grew by $0.95 cents in the first month, and then increased to $1,009.31 in principal for the last month.

So, from the first month, we are earning interest that is paid back to us on the principal paid that month. The interest was converted and paid back to us as principal, which reduced the debt. It becomes a principal payment, reducing the mortgage balance.

This is the first 95 cents earned toward the $107,134 in interest on principal paid. It is interest converted to principal that is credited as principal, so it is tax-free.

LET'S DO AN ADDITIONAL MONTH

To compute the interest earned, you pay the total principal paid monthly at the end of any period and multiply it by 5% or the interest rate on the loan. Remember, our example is using 5% interest, but another loan could be at 3%, 4%, 7%, or 8%. The interest paid on the loan is the interest rate we pay on principal, the total paid for the first 12 months.

To double-check, take the beginning balance of $188,800 multiplied by 5%, and the yearly interest is $9,440.

The mortgage balance, as shown on the amortization schedule for the 12 months (Line 12), is $186,014.51. The interest at 5% would be $186,014.51 x 5% = $9,300.73, or $775.06 a month.

The difference between the beginning mortgage balance and the current mortgage balance after the 12 months is $2,785,49. This represents the principal paid in the first 12 months of the first year.

The difference between the first month and the 13th month is $139.27, which is the interest that would have been paid on the principal paid in the first year of $2,785.49.

Principal paid x 5% = interest

$2,785.49 x 5% = $139.27 or $11.61 a month

So, in the first 12 months, we paid $2,785.49 in principal and earned $139.27 in interest. Every year, this amount will be added to the principal paid amount and the additional month paid from year two on.

Now, for 30 years, we get $139.27 x 30 years = $4,178.10 in interest on the first $2,785.49 paid to the principal in the first year, with the process repeating itself for every month we make our payment. Every year, the balance paid increases as more interest converts to principal and debt is reduced.

You have to appreciate this hard-working, interest-paying savings account called a "mortgage."

Math seems confusing because the concept of paying to earn interest on principals is not widely understood.

But I could not think of another way of explaining without the math.

We all complain about the interest when we buy a home, but a large percentage of the interest is paid back to us as interest on the principal.

It gets better every month, so next month, the interest is paid and converted to principal, and interest is earned as it becomes principal. This goes on until the loan is paid in full.

It's pretty good, but it continues to get better.

If this were a savings account, the interest would be taxable. Since this is a loan, the amortization converts the interest to principal, making it tax-free.

Another way to look at this whole process of amortization is that you paid 5% interest and your mortgage note says "5%," but a significant portion of that is paid back to you as principal through the process of amortization.

It looks like you are paying 5%, and you are, but you are also earning 5% on all principal payments made. So, what is the actual interest cost?

If we divide the interest paid off ($175,066.61) by 360 months, we get an average monthly interest payment of $486.30 or $5,835.55 per year, our actual average cost over 30 years.

If you divide the average interest cost by the $188,800 borrowed from the 5% mortgage, you paid 3.09% interest to the bank and 1.91% to yourself as additional principal.

Remember, amortization converts the interest paid on the principal to additional principal.

In actuality, your 5% mortgage costs you 3.09%. The mortgage does it again. It is a real magic maker in terms of value creation.

SO, YOUR AVERAGE MONTHLY INTEREST PAID OVER 30 YEARS IS $486.30.

You started out paying interest at $786.67 per month but only spent an average of $486.30 for interest. The interest rate on the loan seems like a cost, but we know a large percentage comes back to us as principal.

At least when you make your mortgage payment, you can feel good about the mortgage.

Let's also remember that as you pay down the mortgage balance, more goes to principal and less goes to interest, so your tax savings due to the interest being deducted go down while the principal portion of the payment goes up. In effect, you are paying less interest. Thus, every year, your interest deduction goes down for tax purposes.

That is why some buyers will refinance after 10 to 15 years to increase their tax savings.

If you take the proceeds from refinancing and buy a replacement property, you are increasing your income (due to rent) on the investment property.

What could be better than that?

Remember, your stated interest rate is 5%, but due to interest on the principal, you are paying 5% on balance owed in your monthly payment. Your interest cost goes down and the 5% actually averages out to interest of 3.09%.

Further, you also get a tax refund for an interest expense of 5% paid, meaning you save another 1.05%, which comes back as a tax refund—so, your 5% interest on your loan is further reduced from 3.09% to 2.04% due to the interest being tax-refundable.

Another way to think about it is take 5% Interest times by 28% your tax rate this equals 1.04%. This is what is refundable, thus when subtracted from 3.09% you get rounded 2.05% as an effective rate.

Simply... **wild!**

WHAT WE HAVE LEARNED IN CHAPTERS 13 and 14

1. The mortgage pays you interest just like your savings account but at a much higher rate.
2. The interest paid to you on a mortgage is the same rate as the interest you are paying to the bank.
3. In our example using a $188,800 loan at 5% interest, we paid $175,000 in interest to the lender over 30 years.
4. However, we earned an additional $107,134 in interest that was credited to the principal through the amortization process.
5. The interest we received through the mortgage was tax-free.

6. The amortization schedule shows how, as the principal is paid down monthly, the interest payable the next month also goes down slightly at first, then grows larger over time. That extra interest is the interest that would have been due if no principal payment had been credited the previous month.

7. Line 19 on the rent vs. buy spreadsheet is the starting point, representing the first month's principal payment. Each month, through amortization, it will go up. The difference between the first month and any other month is the amount of interest that has become principal for that month through amortization.

8. The interest earned on the principal paid is considered additional—and therefore, tax-free.

9. Our mortgage note said 5%, and we do pay 5%, but I like to think we are getting part of the interest—so, what is our net interest expense? It is actually less than the 5% stated interest rate.

10. We did the calculation and adjusted the interest cost from 5% to 3.09%. We also got a tax refund on interest, so while the loan may say 5%, we are actually paying closer to 3%.

11. If we add in all the other benefits of ownership, we receive more than we pay.

12. A mortgage is your friend.

CHAPTER 15

THE NINTH WEALTH CREATOR: PREPAYMENT OF PRINCIPAL

Now, we will look at the principal component of the mortgage and how you can increase your returns, savings, and wealth creation through the mortgage.

You have to understand that the way interest is charged on a loan creates an opportunity to save.

I went through the explanation of how interest is charged and how the alleged interest cost is not accurate in the previous chapter to help explain the inner workings of the mortgage and (I hope) make some of the other wealth creators more understandable.

Now, we will see how combining larger principal payments saves more, reduces true interest, and pays the loan off faster.

INTEREST EARNED ON PREPAYMENTS

Let's take what we have learned and create some more wealth faster using the mortgage.

Term Length	30 Years	25 Years	20 Years	15 Years
Monthly P&I	$1,014	$1,104	$1,246	$1,467
Term	360 Months	300 Months	240 Months	180 Months
Total P&I	$365,040	$331,200	$299,040	$264,060
Loan Amount	$188,800	$188,800	$188,800	$188,800
Interest Paid	$176,240	$142,400	$110,240	$75,260
Interest Saved	$0.00 Original Amortization	$33,840	$66,000	$100,980

The chart shows the difference in monthly payments and amortizations for our $188,800 loan. In each case, the interest rate being charged remains the same. We are showing 30, 25, 20, and 15-year terms.

The payment for a 30-year term is $1,014. This is the lowest payment and most extended amortization, so it will have the highest interest expense.

If we add $90 a month to the payment, it will go from $1,014 to $1,104. By paying an extra $90, we will pay off the loan in 25 years.

The payment for a 20-year amortization is $1,246, or an increase of $232 more than the 30-year payment of $1,014.

The 15-year amortization has a payment of $1,467, or an increase over the 30-year amortization payment by $453 monthly. You can clearly see savings of $100,980 over the original 30 years of amortization.

You can see that the 30-year has the lowest payment but the most interest paid, and the 15-year has the highest payment and lowest interest paid.

It makes sense as we borrow the same amount of money in every example. The shorter term means less debt repayment time, so we need higher payments.

The chart also clearly shows how much interest will be saved by making larger payments.

The 25-year payment is an extra $90. Compared to the 30-year amortization, you saved $33,840 in interest. As demonstrated in the table $176,240 - $142,400 = $33,840 in interest saved.

The 20-year amortization is possible because the monthly payment was increased by $232. That extra addition to the monthly payment (again compared to the original principal and interest payment for a 30-year amortization loan) saved $66,000 in interest and paid it off in 20 years.

The 15-year term has an increase in the payment of $453 per month.

The loan is paid off in 15 years and saves $100,980 in interest.

Think of the additional payments to principal as earning additional interest to pay down your loan faster. For example, if you had paid an additional $453 a month to convert your 30-year loan to 15 years, you would save $100,980 in interest while only paying $81,540—a difference of $19,440. Over 15 years, this is an additional $1,296 interest earned per year, or $108 a month.

So, we reduced the term of the loan by making a larger payment. We kept the interest rate the same. The total interest paid automatically went down due to the faster repayment.

HOW DO WE REDUCE THE TERM AND INTEREST PAID?

By making extra principal payments.

If we buy a property, our income taxes go down. If those tax savings are added to our mortgage payment monthly or as a lump sum at the end of the year when we get the tax refund, we go from a 30-year amortization to a 20-year one. By reducing the loan term, this extra payment saves us $66,000 in interest.

So, just committing to paying our tax refund to the principal made a big difference.

Now, consider paying half of every pay raise toward the loan. We may pay an extra $100 or $200 from our pay raises in a few years. So, we have knocked off another 10 years from the amortization.

Could we increase the amount of principal from another source? What if we were to cut our spending on Starbucks Coffee or bring lunch from home to work? A hundred other little changes in our spending habits would save cash that could go to our mortgage payment. Also, working overtime or on holidays may bring in a small amount of extra income, but if it goes to the principal and reduces the term of our loan, we have a bonus of interest savings on the loan.

Adding monthly or yearly amounts is possible if we choose to make the changes and sacrifices necessary in our budget and spending habits to save the needed funds.

We are Americans; if we are good at anything, it is spending money. So, to create wealth and buy a home, practice saving money by spending wisely.

As homeowners save money to pay their mortgage, it makes a lot of sense and accelerates the creation of wealth, and M. F. Day ("Mortgage-Free Day") will come soon.

This also tells you it makes sense to pay additional principal payments as soon as possible so that you can start saving interest on that prepayment amount. You will receive savings on every monthly payment until the loan is paid in full. We know the first year's interest will be a bigger portion of the payment, so making additional prepayments as fast as possible is best—even if it's only a few dollars a month. This is where you obtain the greatest return on each dollar that occurs earlier in terms of interest saved.

INTEREST ON PREPAID PRINCIPAL

So, not only can you see a mortgage as a savings account, it also pays the note rate on all additional payments made in addition to the required payment amounts. In this case, the note interest rate is 5%.

Let's assume you get a $10,000 bonus and want to save it, so you open a savings account paying 5% interest. You will earn $500 a year in interest, but you must pay taxes on the interest income. If you prepay your loan (which is 5% in our example), then by $10,000, you will earn $500 interest a year and shorten your loan term, but its interest is tax-free since, by definition, it's converted to principal. That yearly interest is not a one-time saving; you will get it yearly for the term remaining on the loan.

While you may earn $500 per year, this is also taxable income, so you will have to deduct the taxes to get a true picture of what your return is. Taxes in our examples have been 20% to 30%.

So, taxes take away $100 to $150.

Now, suppose you have a loan at 5% and pay the $10,000 as an additional principal payment. In that case, you earn 5% since that is the interest that would have been paid if the payment had not been made, so you pay no taxes because it is classified as principal, and that money you kept instead of paying taxes is earning interest.

It can't get any better than that.

Interest is calculated on the remaining balance, and you reduce the outstanding balance by $10,000 by making the payment.

So, if I paid the $10,000 in the first month, we would save $500 a year for 30 years. You don't get a check for $500 yearly; instead, it is credited monthly to the principal on your loan through amortization.

In this example, I paid for it in the first month, so we still have 360 months of payments to make. Another way to say this would be that we save $15,000 in interest for the whole term of the loan, or 30 years. Either way, the mortgage amortization process paid us interest rather than us paying the bank interest on the $10,000.

All that math helps you realize prepayments, earn interest, and save on future and total interest costs. Those extra payments will bring you closer to a debt-free, no-mortgage payment heaven.

We make extra principal payments to earn interest on that payment and reduce the term of the loan.

Paying a 30-year amortized loan in 10 to 20 years is possible.

Most mortgage loans will allow you to prepay up to 20% yearly of the original amount borrowed with no prepayment penalty.

When choosing a loan, you want one that will allow some prepayment of the loan.

Lenders have a cost to fund a loan and don't want to get paid back too soon, so most loans will allow partial (but not full) prepayment for the first five years.

You can pay extra monthly or in one lump sum if you don't exceed the maximum prepayment allowed.

LOAN TERM

Remember, the monthly payment is based on an interest rate and the loan's terms. The longer the term, the lower the payment.

Conversely, the shorter the term, the higher the payment. Loans are usually amortized for terms of 15 to 30 years.

I recommend the longest term to get the lowest payment. If times are good, you can pay more monthly and the term will be shortened—but if you run into a rough patch, you can return to the lower 30-year payment. If you take a 15-year payment, you must always pay that amount, and you can't go lower if times are tough.

Before closing out this chapter, I want to make an important point: what I champion is *just one* approach.

While it is important for you and your family's planning and strategy, you decide on which approach works best for you, your situation, and your tolerances. However, the approach of prioritizing excess cash toward your mortgage is great for those who need it for reasons such as:

a. Looking for a guaranteed return

b. Have a high mortgage interest rate

c. Want fewer monthly expenses and are perhaps approaching retirement

d. Are risk-averse

We will quickly gloss over approaches that boil down to risk tolerances and objectives that could fill a whole different book.

The approach we champion prioritizes a guaranteed return and pathway to paying off the loan as quickly as possible. Other approaches champion investing excess cash to outgrow the effective mortgage interest rate. Different approaches are a balance of both, with some excess capital put toward the loan and some toward investments or other holdings of greater liquidity.

Consult your tax and estate planning advisory for more information.

SCORECARD OWNER VALUE AND RENTERS' COSTS PICKED UP EARLIER IN A SAVINGS ACCOUNT CALLED "MORTGAGE"

An additional $15,000 in interest was converted to the principal in our example through a prepayment of $10,000, tax-free, and reducing our loan term.

WHAT WE HAVE LEARNED IN CHAPTER 15

1. I encourage all my clients to make additional principal payments on their loans. It should be part of their regular monthly payment, even if it's only a dollar at first.

2. If you change your spending habits (bringing lunch to work, no Starbucks Coffee, etc.) by eliminating or reducing some of your innocent vices, you could save $100 to $200 a month, which could be paid on principal. If you had a 5% interest rate and paid an extra $100, you would save $5 per month in interest.

3. That would be a prepayment of $1,200 to $2,400 a year.

4. We also get a tax refund yearly, which is another $200 to $300 or $2,400 to $3,600 yearly.

5. I recommend you pay at least 50% of any pay raise to the additional principal.

6. If you get a bonus or an inheritance, put at least 50% into the principal.

7. You get the point. We could all pay our loans off faster and save thousands in interest.

8. If you were to add up all those numbers, you could quickly pay an additional $1,500 per month to the principal—and as pay increases, your extra principal could increase.

9. Understanding the first few years of owning is critical, as you pay more to buy than to rent in cash. But after the benefits of owning, the picture changes in your favor. So, having a budget and managing your finances is important. This has to be a team or family project.

10. If you can work overtime on holiday or a second job, that extra income can go to an additional principal payment, reducing your loan term and saving you interest. It is also part of the principal that interest is paid on, so you are earning money on the

extra payment. Thus, a $500 additional payment (if paid on principal) could earn another $1,500 in interest. That $500 may not seem like a lot, but you actually get paid $2,000 for homeownership.

11. There are a number of philosophies and approaches when it comes to additional capital that may be allocated to extra payments on your mortgage, investments, etc. Consult your tax and estate planner advisory to solidify you and your family's game plan.

CHAPTER 16

RENT VS. BUY FOR THE INVESTOR OWNER

We are using a new worksheet for the investor owner and investment properties. The new worksheet is not a comparison of renting to buying, but rather the advantages of an investment property compared to being an owner-occupant or tenant.

Since we started by comparing renting to owning, we will continue with that comparison. However, you will notice much more considerable tax savings for the investor/owner, which means more significant benefits and greater losses or lost opportunities for the tenant.

So, we are still comparing monthly payments for owning and renting. Again, make sure you are using the monthly figure, not the yearly one. A lot of expenses (such as insurance, property taxes, etc.) may be yearly. Our worksheet assumes monthly expenses and income.

You can use it for other periods than monthly. The most logical one would be yearly.

If you use the yearly totals, make sure all totals are yearly and not monthly. Much like how oil and water do not mix, monthly and yearly do not mix either; if mixed, inaccurate numbers will be provided.

Make sure you are consistent on all totals used—both monthly and yearly.

You will notice the enclosed investor worksheet in the back of the book alongside the other accompanying worksheets.

The basic change in the worksheet is the addition of a simple financial statement in Section (D) of the worksheet.

(D) ACTUAL MONTHLY TAX-DEDUCTIBLE EXPENSES

The investor has to claim the rent as income but can deduct all expenses as cost, reducing the taxable income and amount of taxes paid. You will notice that many additional expenses have been added.

Owner-occupants can only deduct specific items while investors are running a rental business, so that they can claim all costs as a business expense. However, they must also claim the rental income as taxable income.

In the earlier sheet, we compared renting to buying. What would happen if the tenant were to purchase as an owner-occupant and the rent was replaced by a monthly mortgage payment?

In this case, you are buying as an investor, so the rental income must be claimed as income. However, you are also able to deduct all expenses associated with ownership and management of your unit. The expenses reduce the taxable income.

Items that an owner-occupant cannot deduct (such as insurance, repairs, maintenance fees, etc.) are deductible for an investor/owner.

The good news is that the same wealth creators for residential owner-occupant buyers are there for investors. So, the formulas and math are the same.

INTRODUCING THE THREE ADDITIONAL INVESTOR WEALTH CREATORS

The investors have three additional wealth creators (shown on the sheet in red).

They are:

1) rental income;

2) deducting rental business operating expenses; and

3) depreciation.

(D) INCOME EXPENSE STATEMENT	
I. Rent Income	_____
II. Expenses	
1. Advertising	_____
2. Cleaning	_____
3. Insurance	_____
4. Legal Fees	_____
5. Maintenance	_____
6. Tax Prep Fee	_____
7. Management Fee	_____
8. Mortgage Interest	_____
9. Repairs	_____
10. Supplies	_____
11. Taxes	_____
12. Utilities	_____
13. Pest Control	_____
14. Painting	_____
15. Plumbing	_____
16. AOUO Fees	_____
17. Total £ Monthly £ Yearly Expenses	_____
18. Depreciation	_____
19. Total Expenses	_____
Total	

Each will be discussed in more detail in the next three chapters—but for now, let me give you a little background on each one.

1. Rent is the income created by the tenant paying rent to the landlord. The investor's rental income can be used to help pay the cost of mortgage ownership, including the mortgage.

2. Deducting rental business operating expenses means that by buying a rental property, you have started a small business of renting a home to make a profit or create income and value. The expenses include all costs to operate your rental business. Most costs are directly tied to the property. The money you spend on the property can also include the cost of managing the property. Keep track of rental income and all checks written to pay expenses. If you mail the mortgage payment, the stamp and envelope are a cost and tax-deductible.

   The list within Section D gives you a good idea of the expenses that can be tax-deductible. It is not a complete list, but it covers most of the obvious cost categories. The best (and most complex) expense is depreciation.

3. Depreciation is taken only on the value of the improvements. So, you take the total purchase price and subtract the land value. The balance remaining is the portion of the purchase price that can be depreciated.

Usually, that value has to be spread over the anticipated life of the improvements. For a newer home, this would be 30 to 40 years. The longer the life, the lower the yearly deduction. For depreciation, you want the shortest period of time, which will give you the largest deduction. Ask your tax consultant if you have questions or look at the IRS' depreciation pamphlets and other real estate topics. You should be able to access them online, and they are free.

Please realize that there are many advantages to investment properties, but this is not a book about investing; it is limited to the wealth creators in real estate, as shown in the rent vs. own worksheet.

You can see a blank, with arrows pointing to the wealth creators and filled-out worksheet for investors on the following pages.

WORKSHEET SHOWING INVESTOR WEALTH CREATORS

<u>RENT-VS-BUY WORKSHEET</u>
INVESTOR (Showing Wealth Creators)

FOR: _____   (1) Time   **DATE:** _____

(A) PROPERTY DESCRIPTION		BUY	
I. Description: _____		(2) Receiving Rent (Refer to "D," below)	
II. Location:			
III. Land Tenure:	Fee Simple		
IV. Down Payment:	____ %		
V. Financing Terms:	1st Mortgage: ___-Year Mortgage / ___% Interest		
VI. Tax Assumptions:	Owner-Occupant Using Itemized Deductions		

(B) FINANCING TERMS		
1. Sales Price of Home		(3) Appreciation
2. Cash Required for Down Payment		(4) Leverage
3. Mortgage		(5) Savings Account
4. Other		

(C) MONTHLY PAYMENT		
5. Principal and Interest (P & I)		(6) Constant Monthly Payment
(Line 5 - Line 11 = Principal)		
6. Deposit for Property Taxes (Approximate)		
7. Mortgage Insurance - Lender		
8. Maintenance Payments (AOUA)		
9. Other: _____		
10. Total Monthly Payments		

(D) INCOME EXPENSE STATEMENT		
I. Rent Income		(10) Income
II. Expenses		(11) Expense
1. Advertising		
2. Cleaning		
3. Insurance		
4. Legal Fees		
5. Maintenance		
6. Tax Prep Fee		
7. Management Fee		
8. Mortgage Interest		
9. Repairs		
10. Supplies		
11. Taxes		
12. Utilities		
13. Pest Control		
14. Painting		
15. Plumbing		
16. AOUO Fees		
17. Total £ Monthly £ Yearly Expenses		
18. Depreciation		(12) Depreciation
19. Total Expenses		
Total		

Depreciation: Sales Price - Land Value = Depreciable Improvements | We Assume a 33 Year Life (Could be longer or shorter)

(E) CASH SAVINGS PER MONTH ON TAXES	
(TAX BRACKET % x TOTAL DEDUCTIONS AS SHOWN ON LINE 12)	(7) Tax Deduction Including Depreciation
15. 31% Tax Bracket ($____ x 31%) Line 19 x 31% =	
16. 28% Tax Bracket ($____ x 28%) Line 19 x 28% =	
17. 15% Tax Bracket ($____ x 15%) Line 19 x 15% =	

(F) DETERMINING ACTUAL MONTHLY COST OF BUYING				
(WHEN ADJUSTED FOR TAX & EQUITY PAID)				
	31%	28%	15%	
18. Total Monthly Payment (Line 10)				
19. Subtract Cash Savings on Taxes				
(Line 15, Line 16, or Line 17)				
20. Monthly Payment Adjusted for Tax Savings				
21. Subtract EQUITY Portion of Monthly Payment				(8) Principal
(Equity or Principal = Line 5 Minus Interest x Line 11)				
22. Actual Monthly Payment				
			What You Are Paying to Own	What You Are Paying to Rent

(G) DIFFERENT MONTHLY PAYMENTS BASED ON AMORTIZATION					
Comparison of Payments and Amortization				(9) Prepayment	
	Payment Option 1: 30 Yr	Payment Option 2: 25 Yr	Difference Option 1	Payment Option 3: 20 Yr	Difference Option 1
Monthly Principal & Interest:					
x Term of Loan in Months					
"= Total Principal & Interest					
- Beginning Mortgage Balance					
"= Interest Paid					

WORKSHEET FOR INVESTOR FILLED OUT

RENT-VS-BUY WORKSHEET
INVESTOR

FOR: _____   DATE: _____

(A) PROPERTY DESCRIPTION		BUY	RENT
I. Description:	2-Bedroom /1-Bath		$ 1 200
II. Location:	Plantation Town Apartments, Unit 707		
III. Land Tenure:	Fee Simple		
IV. Down Payment:	20%		
V. Financing Terms:	1st Mortgage: 30-Year Mortgage / 5% Interest		
VI. Tax Assumptions:	Owner-Occupant Using Itemized Deductions		

(B) FINANCING TERMS

1.	Sales Price of Home	$ 236 000
2.	Cash Required for Down Payment	$ 47 200
3.	Mortgage	$ 188 800
4.	Other	$ -

(C) MONTHLY PAYMENT

5.	Principal and Interest (P & I) (Line 5 - Line 11 = Principal)	$ 1 014,00
6.	Deposit for Property Taxes (Approximate)	$ 72,00
7.	Mortgage Insurance - Lender	
8.	Maintenance Payments (AOUA)	$ 255,00
9.	Other: _____	$ -
10.	**Total Monthly Payments**	$ 1 341,00

(D) INCOME EXPENSE STATEMENT

I. Rent Income		$ 1 200,00
II. Expenses		
	Advertising	
	Cleaning	
	Insurance	20,00
	Legal Fees	
	Maintenance	
	Tax Prep Fee	
	Management Fee	120,00
	Mortgage Interest	787,00
	Repairs	
	Supplies	
	Taxes	72,00
	Utilities	
	Pest Control	
	Painting	
	Plumbing	
	AOUO Fees	225,00

(Prin. & Int.)   (Int.)   (Prin.)
Line 11: $1,014 - $787 = $227

Total £ Monthly £ Yearly Expenses	$ <1,152.00>
Depreciation	$ < 295.00>
Total	$ 1,447.00

Depreciation: Sales Price - Land Value = Depreciable Improvements	We Assume a 33 Year Life
$236,000 - $100,000 = $136,000	$136,000 , 33 Years = $3,540 Per Year , 12 = $295 Per Month

(E) CASH SAVINGS PER MONTH ON TAXES
(TAX BRACKET % x TOTAL DEDUCTIONS AS SHOWN ON LINE 12)

15. 31% Tax Bracket ($1,447 x 31%) Line 14 x 31%	=	$ 448,57
16. 28% Tax Bracket ($1,447 x 28%) Line 14 x 28%	=	$ 405,16
17. 15% Tax Bracket ($1,447 x 15%) Line 14 x 15%	=	$ 217,05

(F) DETERMINING ACTUAL MONTHLY COST OF BUYING
(WHEN ADJUSTED FOR TAX & EQUITY PAID)

	31%	28%	15%		
18. Total Monthly Payment (Line 10)	$ 1 341	$ 1 341	$ 1 341		
19. Subtract Cash Savings on Taxes (Line 15, Line 16, or Line 17)	$ 448	$ 405	$ 217		$ 241
20. Monthly Payment Adjusted for Tax Savings	$ 893	$ 936	$ 1 124		
21. Subtract EQUITY Portion of Monthly Payment (Equity or Principal = Line 5 Minus Interest x Line 11)	$ 227	$ 227	$ 227		$ 227
22. **Actual Monthly Payment**	$ 666	$ 709	$ 897	$ 848 to $ 985	$ 1 668
				What You Are Paying to Own	What You Are Paying to Rent

WHAT WE HAVE LEARNED IN CHAPTER 16

1. We were introduced to three new wealth creators that become available if we decide to buy rental properties as an investment.

2. The nine existing wealth creators in real estate still apply, and three more have been added to that list.

3. I am using a simple income and expense statement for this exercise.

4. If you decide to start with an investment apartment or buy one after a few years, the benefits of being an investor are important. *(*Note: I was able to live at home and was fortunate enough to team up with my sister and buy my first unit when I was 15 years old. By the time I moved out at the age of 25, I owned four units before buying my first apartment to live in.)*

5. The new form looks similar to the first, but it is actually different. In the residential form, we dealt with or looked at items that were deductible for the owner-occupied, basically property, taxes, interest, and mortgage insurance premiums. Now, we are looking at an investor renting out a unit or building. Thus, we now have to account for the rental income, which is taxable to the unit owner or landlord owner.

6. We can also add in the other expenses an investor may have. Every expense the owner has is deductible. This would include all the deductions of the owner-occupant, but also provides water, electricity, land, lease rent, insurance, advertising, repairs, maintenance, etc. In effect, every expense associated with that property advertising gas for your car because you're driving to show the property to potential renters, expense to your new business landlord. Remember, the owner-occupant pays a maintenance fee. Pay water pays. Electricity pays all the same expenses but cannot deduct them because he is not an investor; he is an owner-occupant.

7. So, we have modified the form to show the addition of the rental income and a list of possible expenses. The concept is the same. While the property creates benefits for an owner-occupant, it creates even more benefits for an investor. *(*Note: When I first started out in real estate, I did not start as an occupant. I started as an investor, buying a property to rent. I was living at home at that point and saw no sense in having to make a mortgage payment as an owner-occupant when I could do it as an investor, collect the rent, and deduct all the expenses. I mentioned this: everyone looks to buy a home to live in when it might sometimes be a better move to purchase an investment property—especially if you're living in a low-rent unit or at home.)*

CHAPTER 17

RENTAL INCOME

The investor's 10th wealth creator is the rental income they receive as the landlord. We removed the rental column at the far right for the price on the enclosed investor worksheet *(see snippet below).*

RENT-VS-BUY WORKSHEET
INVESTOR (Showing Wealth Creators)

FOR: _____   (1) Time **DATE:** _____

(A) PROPERTY DESCRIPTION		BUY
I. Description: _____	(2) Receiving Rent (Refer to "DI" below)	
II. Location: _____		
III. Land Tenure: Fee Simple		
IV. Down Payment: _____%		
V. Financing Terms: 1st Mortgage: ___-Year Mortgage / ___% Interest		
VI. Tax Assumptions: Owner-Occupant Using Itemized Deductions		

(B) FINANCING TERMS		
1. Sales Price of Home _____	(3) Appreciation	
2. Cash Required for Down Payment _____	(4) Leverage	
3. Mortgage _____	(5) Savings Account	
4. Other _____		

(C) MONTHLY PAYMENT		
5. Principal and Interest (P & I)	(6) Constant Monthly Payment _____	
(Line 5 - Line 11 = Principal)		
6. Deposit for Property Taxes (Approximate)		_____
7. Mortgage Insurance - Lender		_____
8. Maintenance Payments (AOUA)		_____
9. Other: _____		_____
10. Total Monthly Payments		_____

(D) INCOME EXPENSE STATEMENT		
I. Rent Income _____		
II. Expenses		
1. Advertising		_____
2. Cleaning		_____
3. Insurance		_____
4. Legal Fees		_____
5. Maintenance		

The rent is now picked up in Section D, along with all the expenses. *(*Note: you can find the complete form in the back under "TABLES & WORKSHEETS.")* The format is a simple income and expenses statement for the property. The income is shown first; then, all the expenses are shown and deducted from the income. Depreciation is an accounting concept that results in additional expenses, creating another deduction. Depreciation is a bonus since no cash is spent to create the expense. For all the other deductions, you had to spend money. Depreciation is an accounting concept of only the value of the improvements, not the land. The improvements lose value through age and/or become obsolete.

If you look at all the expense items, you will see that (like an owner-occupied home) you get to deduct the interest, property taxes, and mortgage insurance. Those expenses are found in Section D.

You will notice we have a complete list of costs and expenses. By buying an investment property, you are opening a small business and renting out the unit.

All costs associated with that business are tax deductible—the condo maintenance fee, electricity, water, as well as if the landlord pays, advertising, repairs, etc.

In my case, I purchased an investment property first before buying a home. I owned an interest in a number of units before I was 20. I bought my first unit at 15 with money saved from my newspaper route and odd jobs.

Since I was living at home, it made more sense to buy an investment property. I was too young to own, so I teamed up with my sister (who had just gotten a job as a teacher), and we purchased a one-bedroom apartment in Waikiki.

We both lived at home, so renting it out made sense.

If you find yourself in a situation where you are living at home and happy or have an outstanding rental deal, don't give that up just to become an owner-occupant.

Use that period to your advantage, save as much cash as possible, and consider buying an investment property and renting it out. Remember, any extra money you accrue by living at home or paying low rent can be used to reduce your debt on the investment property.

It may be easier to qualify since you have your employment income and can also claim the rent as additional income to make qualifying easier.

A lot of the time, you can find a home or property that has a rental unit, living in one or renting both out.

A duplex, triplex, or fourplex may qualify as a single-family home for financing. So, if a family wants to buy (your parents or brother and sister are going to buy together), then you should ask your realtor to show you those options. It is like buying a small apartment building for a family or group of friends.

If you start with a home to live in first as an owner-occupant, then you may want to refinance and release cash to buy the new property. If you own two properties, you are an investor—an investor/landlord for the rental property and an owner-occupant for the unit you live in.

So, the first benefit of being a landlord is that you are able to charge rent. You will have obligations to pay the cost of ownership (including the mortgage), but it does not come from your employment income; it comes from rental income. Being a landlord is having another monthly payday: a check from your tenants paying their rent.

You now have 12 wealth creators working for you, and if you own two properties, you are doubling up on the wealth creators; you get up to 12 wealth creators working for you. Remember, the newest three wealth creators available on the investment property are not available to the residential owner-occupant, but only to the investor.

As an investor, you get to use 100% of the residential wealth creators plus the three available to the investor.

The first one (income) is self-explanatory, as it gives you another paycheck or income to help with the payment—and if you're lucky, you may even have a positive cash flow. This means that after all expenses are paid, there is money left over. The rent is taxable as additional income on state and federal taxes. But do not worry; just like other aspects of real estate, the extra benefits will usually reduce or eliminate tax liability.

If you are becoming a first-time investor, you should hire a realtor rental management company and agent to manage the rental property.

As an active real estate developer, I *know* it is not advisable to try and do it yourself. Some of the perks of having a professional management company handle it are that they will take care of late-night calls, maintenance, tenant affairs and relations, leasing efforts, and preparation of reports for tax professionals, as well as navigate the laws on your behalf that clarify the relationships between landlords and tenants and shield you from some legal pitfalls in the event that something goes sideways. They are appropriately insured to conduct real estate transactions because that is what they do day in and day out. Thus, unless you have that experience, I would steer *clear*.

In short, hire a professional rental management company to help manage the rental. Of course, this is a *shameless self-promotion warning*. I recommend making use of our services, Savio Asset Management, in our Savio Group of Companies.

In our first few chapters, we looked at how much rent is paid. As a renter, it was terrible news. As an investor, however, rent becomes good news and helps create more wealth for you as the property owner.

Renting is supposed to be a chance for tenants to save funds so that they can buy.

As a small first-time investor, this is a chance for you to get ahead, but it does not mean you cannot help your tenant.

As a landlord, I want enough rent to pay the mortgage and the cost of owning the property. As a rule, my rents would be below market since I knew I was making money through the wealth creators. I was willing to give my tenants a break in the form of lower rent. I also hoped to get a better tenant who would stay longer, and I would have fewer vacancies and lower rent costs. Today, I would like to do one additional favor for my tenant: I would give him a copy of my book and tell him he should try and buy a home for his family and their future.

Being an investor is not about money, but rather about solving problems efficiently and helping people. The money will follow.

As an aside, I am working on a rent-to-build equity program where I will rent to tenants—and then after, say, ten years of renting, I will give them back all the value the wealth creators have generated as long as they use the funds to buy a home. You should not be as generous as I am because you are just starting. But when you are older and financially comfortable, do something good for your community.

Helping others is what American capitalism is all about.

CHAPTER 18

BUSINESS EXPENSES

The real estate investor's 11th wealth creator is *deducting expenses.* As an investor, you have started your own little business. As a business, you have to claim the rent as income so that you can deduct the corresponding expenses. Under the federal tax code and most state tax codes, the expenses would be all costs associated with the ownership of the investment property.

As an owner-occupant of a single-family home, you could deduct interest, property taxes, and lender mortgage insurance fees.

As an investor/owner and landlord, you can deduct all costs of operating your rental unit business as a business expense.

In the investor's rent vs. buy worksheet, Section D is different and now has a simple financial sheet where you can show monthly rental income and the monthly expenses, which represent payments made for the operation of the property. You are spending a dollar to save a percentage of that expense in taxes.

As an investor, you can deduct all costs of your rental unit (see snippet).

```
(D)  INCOME EXPENSE STATEMENT
     I. Rent Income                           _____
    II. Expenses
          1.  Advertising                          _____
          2.  Cleaning                             _____
          3.  Insurance                            _____
          4.  Legal Fees                           _____
          5.  Maintenance                          _____
          6.  Tax Prep Fee                         _____
          7.  Management Fee                       _____
          8.  Mortgage Interest                    _____
          9.  Repairs                              _____
         10.  Supplies                             _____
         11.  Taxes                                _____
         12.  Utilities                            _____
         13.  Pest Control                         _____
         14.  Painting                             _____
         15.  Plumbing                             _____
         16.  AOUO Fees                            _____
         17.  Total £ Monthly  £ Yearly  Expenses  _____
         18.  Depreciation                     _____
         19.  Total Expenses                   _____
                                    Total
```

This includes things such as interest, property taxes, insurance, water, electricity, repairs, maintenance fees if condo, advertising, accounting, property management, legal fees, advertising, tax preparation, yard work, and all costs.

Your deductions are much more inclusive, so your tax savings will be much more significant than they would for an owner-occupied residential unit.

You must keep good records to prove the expenses to your account and the IRS if you are audited.

If you invest in an apartment or home to rent, you should open a checking account to deposit all the income, and you should write all the checks to pay the expenses. If you are audited by the IRS or need the records, they will be in one place. *Consult your CPA for more information regarding dollars spent vs. dollars saved in tax reductions that may be available to you given your locality at the city, county, state, and federal levels. They will be aware of present, pending, and recent changes.*

Furthermore, if you are a new landlord, as said previously, there is nothing wrong with hiring a company to manage for you—especially if you are unfamiliar with county, state, and federal housing laws. *In*

FACT, I highly advise it. Again, the realtor that helped you can also recommend a property management company to you.

WHAT WE HAVE LEARNED IN CHAPTER 18

1. We learned that owning an investment creates tax-deductible business expenses.

2. We learned that the deductions help offset the taxable rental income we receive.

3. All expenses (such as interest, property taxes, insurance, advertising, accounting, repairs, tax advice, preparation of tax returns, legal fees, property management fees, etc.) are deductible.

4. Every dollar we spend eats up a dollar we earn in rent.

5. Keeping good records is important.

CHAPTER 19

DEPRECIATION

The investor's 12th wealth creator, depreciation is a tax shelter or loss created by the federal tax code and standard accounting procedure. Basically, it assumes all manufactured or man-made products have a cost and life expectancy.

Definition of Depreciation

The one real bonus in investing in real estate is depreciation. You spend nothing but get to depreciate or take the value of the improvements (the man-made portions of the property, not the land) as an expense.

In our example, we calculate depreciation over a 27.5 year life. The property is $236,000. The land = $100,000 and the building/improvements = $136,600.

$136,600 of depreciable improvements/building

/ (divided by) 27.5 years

= $4,945 in eligible depreciation per year

Then you calculate your reduction based on your combined state and federal taxes. In our example we use 31%, 28% and 15%.

Tax Reduction would be $4,945. x (your combined tax bracket).

If, 28%, your tax reduction is $1,385 annualized, broken monthly $115. *Note*, numbers are rounded.

Now, let's return to the concept of depreciation.

Depreciation is an accounting or paper loss, but not a true dollar or cash expense or loss. For your other expenses, you spend a dollar and get back a portion of it through a tax deduction and refund. Let's say your tax bracket is 15% to 40%; you would get that percentage back in the form of a tax refund. So, you spend a dollar and get back 15 to 40 cents of every dollar spent on the property. That is better than nothing, and a great benefit; with depreciation, however, you pay nothing but get to claim the value of improvements, which are losing value over time.

So, a dollar of depreciation shelters one dollar of income. You get the depreciation for free since it is an accounting concept, so it is better than spending a dollar to get back a portion of a dollar.

You get the deduction but don't have to spend the money.

The key is that it is a bookkeeping entry and does not cost you anything.

Meanwhile, interest costs a dollar. Property taxes cost a dollar.

Everything costs something, and Uncle Sam gives you back a percentage of that. However, depreciation is an accounting assumption. Everything indeed grows old, and will lose its value and/or need to be repaired or replaced at some point.

Our home in Honolulu is a good example. My wife and I purchased it for $290,000 in 1990. The value was allocated 50% to land and 50% to the improvements (the house). It was about 40 years old at that point.

Today, our home is worth $2,000,000. The house is worth $300,000, and the land is worth $1.7 million.

The home is still completely livable. It is concrete, so if we were ever to sell, a new buyer could keep the home and build a second floor.

If this was not our home but an investment property, we could depreciate the value of the improvements over a 30- to 40-year period.

If the building is valued at $500,000 and has an expected life of 30 years, we could claim a depreciation expense of $16,666 per year.

Unlike other expenses, it did not cost us money; it is a hypothetical expense that we can take as a tax loss. If we are in a 30% tax bracket and apply that tax rate to the yearly depreciation of $16,666, we will save $4,999.80 in taxes that year. Most (if not all) would go to paying off debt as a once-a-year lump sum payment on the principal.

That depreciation loss generated for taxes is a paper loss of value. This is possible because the tax code allows the depreciation of the improvement's value as a reasonable business expense.

Notice that the land is forever and has gone up in value over 30-plus years of ownership.

Depreciation is a bonus to owners, so use it to your advantage and create wealth for the future using its tax-saving power wisely.

In summary, for the last 3 chapters as they are geared towards the investor owner. The total benefits to the landlord is they get rent plus all the other benefits of owning, plus the depreciation.

Using our forms, you can calculate the cash and non-cash benefits, to determine tax savings, non-cash benefits, after tax cash impact and total financial impact. Though we will move on from there for a deeper analysis of investing can be a compendium of other books unto itself. Never know, perhaps in our next book we will tackle that.

WHAT WE HAVE LEARNED IN CHAPTER 19

1. We learned that depreciation is a tax deduction available ONLY to the investor owner, whereby the owner does not have to spend any money to reap the benefit.

2. We also learned that in other deductions (such as what we learned from the prior chapter on business expenses), you can take many more deductions compared to owner-occupants and get a percentage of each dollar earned back. However, each is generated from actual dollars spent, compared to depreciation, leading into our third point.

3. Depreciation is an accounting entry and costs NOTHING, but it can generate substantial tax savings to create additional opportunities with the capital saved through said reductions.

4. We have learned to use it when applicable.

CHAPTER 20

A CALL TO ACTION

Now, you have a better understanding of real estate and how value is created through ownership. If you are happy renting, no further action is required. But if you are thinking of buying or have decided to buy, what should you do? What action do you take to become a homeowner?

Do what the book says: take the first wealth creator (time) to decide where you are and what needs to be done.

Everyone is going to be a little different, but certain things should be considered.

1. I assume you read the book and have an understanding of why you should buy, as well as what to expect in creating wealth.

2. You should take the time to inventory where you are. Is your family in agreement? Get the family to read and understand the concepts. We need the family to work as a team. Sacrifices may be required, and so it's important to ensure they are on board. If alone, then you need to be sure you are committed and ready to make the necessary sacrifices to become a homeowner.

3. Take the time to look at your finances—bills, monthly obligations, etc. What are you paying in rent? What can you afford to pay toward a mortgage? Do you have funds for a down payment or closing costs?

4. Take the time to get prequalified for a loan. Do you qualify for no money down financing? Does someone in your family qualify? Can you partner with them? Does your state have programs available to help renters buy?

5. Work on preparing a budget so that you know where you presently spend your money. Can you tighten up or save on certain items or activities? Let's assume you buy a coffee every morning at Starbucks for $5, which is $25 per week or $100 per month. If you buy your coffee at McDonald's or bring one from home to save up to $100 a month, you can use that amount to make an additional principal payment. The same is true for lunches, dinners, etc. Really think about what you can give up with the idea of being debt-free in 10 to 15 years.

6. If your employment is secure, is there potential for advancement?

7. Check to see whether your community has home-bought classes. You and your spouse or partner should go. They can be private or government-sponsored.

8. Start looking at prices and neighborhoods, and remember the steppingstone approach—buy what you can afford and are comfortable with, and move up over time.

9. Nothing can destroy the fun of creating wealth faster than being too aggressive on your acquisition, taking too much risk, and saddling yourself with too much debt and a payment you can't afford to make.

10. Find a realtor in your area that you are comfortable with and who works with first-time buyers. Ask if he has read the book. At least you will be speaking the same language and understand the concepts.

11. Go look at open houses to get a sense of the market.

12. Again, sit down and talk to family and review what you have learned. This is a team effort.

13. Make a list of things that are important to you in a home and neighborhood you would like to live in.

14. Buy what you like and need, not what you think you like.

15. The first step is essential, so be cautious but firm in taking action.

16. Review the book and the rent vs. buy worksheet to remind yourself that knowledge is confidence.

17. If you have low rent or live at home free, look at buying an investment property and continuing to live where you are.

18. A residential property is defined for lending as up to four units, so you can buy a duplex and still be an owner-occupant.

19. If you start with an investment property, consider hiring a rental agent.

20. In a few years, sell, refinance, and start the process all over again. Repeat as often as needed, as long as you are having fun doing it.

21. If you are successful (and you should be), then help your community, school, or church as much as you can afford to. Share your good fortune and hard work with others.

22. Let your children be part of this adventure. It is being done for their future.

23. If the kids come after success, tell them the story of the book that said you could be a homeowner. Make sure they are prepared to make the sacrifices needed to be successful.

24. Help others and do good.

25. Don't get discouraged. You can do it.

26. If success is worthwhile, it is worth fighting for. Don't get discouraged; once again, YOU CAN DO IT!

Before I go...

The key to ownership is to commit to an understanding of how a mortgage works. Whether you're an owner, occupant, or investor does not matter. The mortgage is going to work for you and your family.

Once you've committed to the mortgage, you also want to commit to making extra payments every chance you get.

It may be $5, $10, or a few hundred dollars ($500). The amount doesn't matter. It may be every month or every other month. That does not matter. What's important is that you commit whenever possible to pay extra amounts toward your mortgage. It may be money you saved from cutting out dinners, a beer after work, or not buying a Starbucks Coffee. All those little savings (or $5 a day) could add up to hundreds of dollars per month that could be paid on your loan over its term, reducing the amount of interest you pay and starting to create wealth.

If you get a pay raise, you should plan on 50% of the net pay raise going to reduce your debt as an additional principal payment. You can pay more if you want, but a minimum of 50% of any pay raise should go to reduce debt.

If you get a bonus for Christmas, or just for work well done or a successful year, I would again put 50% toward the principal as a minimum.

If you get a tax refund at the end of the year, again, I would put (all or a minimum of 50%) toward the principal on the loan.

This type of commitment keeps your mission of reducing debt, saving interest, and reducing the term of your loan at the forefront of the decisions you make. If it encourages you to reduce spending, save more money, or make little sacrifices, that can be fun when you realize you're creating wealth and a future for yourself and your family.

Creating wealth can be easy and fun if the whole family gets involved and makes the commitment. It should be relatively easy to succeed in creating wealth. It can be done. It has been done. I have seen hundreds (if not thousands) of my clients buy properties, when I knew they knew they were going to struggle, but they also knew they would succeed. These clients who bought homes from me 20 to 30 years ago are now multimillionaires. They did what I recommended, paid off their homes as quickly as possible, and at some point, refinanced and purchased a second, third, or even fourth property.

To call it a wrap, I do indeed hope you enjoyed this book! I hope you learned something new, and I encourage you to give it a try. Home-ownership is your future and your family's future, and you can do it. Good luck, and God bless you, your family, and your endeavor to find a home and future!

EPILOGUE

f you've made it this far, thank you, and mahalo! When I first started this journey, I thought I might be losing my mind. But I'm glad to have persevered, and I hope you have too! My goal was to provide a down-to-earth explanation of how real estate not only creates wealth but also generates lasting wealth for future generations. *Hopefully*, that expectation was met.

In addition, I've included a variety of worksheets to help you assess and evaluate wealth-building opportunities—whether you're a first-time homebuyer, looking for a second home, or an investor.

I'd also like to extend my heartfelt thanks to everyone and every experience that has contributed to what I hope are valuable and actionable insights. This book is a reflection of my years as a developer here in Hawaii, and I'm excited to share those insights with you.

Here's a short list of people I'd like to thank for their support in making this book possible and for instilling in me the knowledge I'm now sharing with you.

- ❖ My family and wife, Phyllis Savio.
- ❖ My mother, Mary Savio, with whom I first began my journey at Tropic Shores Realty.
- ❖ Jameson Dahl, my chief contributor, co-conspirator, and all-around "get it done" guy.

TABLES & WORKSHEETS

❖ RENT VS. BUY WS **OWNER-OCCUPANT BLANK**

❖ RENT VS. BUY WS **OWNER-OCCUPANT _(FILLED OUT)_**

❖ RENT VS. BUY WS **OWNER-OCCUPANT _(BLANK, SHOWING WEALTH CREATORS)_**

❖ RENT VS. BUY **INVESTOR WS BLANK SHOWING WEALTH CREATORS**

❖ RENT VS. BUY **INVESTOR WS _(FILLED OUT)_**

❖ AMORTIZATION TABLES

RENT-VS-BUY WORKSHEET
OWNER-OCCUPANT

FOR: _____   DATE: _____

(A) PROPERTY DESCRIPTION		BUY	RENT
I. Description:	_____		
II. Location:	_____		
III. Land Tenure:	_____		
IV. Down Payment:	_____		
V. Financing Terms:	_____		
VI. Tax Assumptions:	_____		

(B) FINANCING TERMS

1. Sales Price of Home	_____	
2. Cash Required for Down Payment	_____	
3. Mortgage	_____	
4. Other	_____	

(C) MONTHLY PAYMENT

5. Principal and Interest (P & I) (Line 5 - Line 11 = Principal)		_____
6. Deposit for Property Taxes (Approximate)		_____
7. Mortgage Insurance - Lender		_____
8. Maintenance Payments (AOUA)		_____
9. Other: _____		_____
10. Total Monthly Payments		_____

(D) ACTUAL MONTHLY TAX DEDUCTIBLE EXPENSES

Homeowner's Tax Deductible Expenses

11. First Month's Interest (Line 3 x Interest Rate ÷ 12 = Interest Per Month)	_____
12. Monthly Tax Deposit	_____
13. Mortgage Insurance	_____
14. Total Deductions	_____

(E) CASH SAVINGS PER MONTH ON TAXES
(TAX BRACKET % x TOTAL DEDUCTIONS AS SHOWN ON LINE 12)

15. 31% Tax Bracket ($____ x 31%) Line 14 x 31% =	_____
16. 28% Tax Bracket ($____ x 28%) Line 14 x 28% =	_____
17. 15% Tax Bracket ($___ x 15%) Line 14 x 15% =	_____

(F) DETERMINING ACTUAL MONTHLY COST OF BUYING
(WHEN ADJUSTED FOR TAX & EQUITY PAID)

	31%	28%	15%		
18. Total Monthly Payment (Line 10)	_____	_____	_____		
19. Subtract Cash Savings on Taxes (Line 15, Line 16, or Line 17)	_____	_____	_____		
20. Monthly Payment Adjusted for Tax Savings	_____	_____	_____		
21. Subtract EQUITY Portion of Monthly Payment (Equity or Principal = Line 5 Minus Interest x Line 11)	_____	_____	_____		
22. Actual Monthly Payment	_____	_____	_____		
				What You Are Paying to Own	What You Are Paying to Rent

(G) DIFFERENT MONTHLY PAYMENTS BASED ON AMORTIZATION

Comparison of Payments and Amortization

	Payment Option 1: 30 Yr	Payment Option 2: 25 Yr	Difference Option 1	Payment Option 3: 20 Yr	Difference Option 1
Monthly Principal & Interest:					
x Term of Loan in Months					
"= Total Principal & Interest					
- Beginning Mortgage Balance					
"= Interest Paid					

RENT-VS-BUY WORKSHEET
OWNER-OCCUPANT

FOR: _____   DATE: _____

(A) PROPERTY DESCRIPTION		BUY	RENT
I. Description:	2-Bedroom /1-Bath	$	1,200
II. Location:	Plantation Town Apartments		
III. Land Tenure:	Fee Simple		
IV. Down Payment:	20%		
V. Financing Terms:	1st Mortgage: 30-Year Mortgage / 5% Interest		
VI. Tax Assumptions:	Owner-Occupant Using Itemized Deductions		

(B) FINANCING TERMS		
1. Sales Price of Home	$	236,000
2. Cash Required for Down Payment	$	47,200
3. Mortgage	$	188,800
4. Other	$	-

(C) MONTHLY PAYMENT			
5. Principal and Interest (P & I)		$	1,014.00
(Line 5 - Line 11 = Principal)			
6. Deposit for Property Taxes (Approximate)		$	72.00
7. Mortgage Insurance - Lender			
8. Maintenance Payments (AOUO)		$	255.00
9. Other: _____		$	-
10. Total Monthly Payments		$ 1,341.00	$1200

(D) ACTUAL MONTHLY TAX DEDUCTIBLE EXPENSES		
Homeowner's Tax Deductible Expenses		
11. First Month's Interest	$	787
(Line 3 x Interest Rate / 12 = Interest Per Month)		
12. Monthly Tax Deposit	$	72
13. Mortgage Insurance		
14. Total Deductions	$	859

(E) CASH SAVINGS PER MONTH ON TAXES		
(TAX BRACKET % x TOTAL DEDUCTIONS AS SHOWN ON LINE 12)		
15. 31% Tax Bracket ($____ x 31%) Line 14 x 31% =	$	266
16. 28% Tax Bracket ($____ x 28%) Line 14 x 28% =	$	241
17. 15% Tax Bracket ($___ x 15%) Line 14 x 15% =	$	129

(F) DETERMINING ACTUAL MONTHLY COST OF BUYING
(WHEN ADJUSTED FOR TAX & EQUITY PAID)

	31%	28%	15%		
18. Total Monthly Payment (Line 10)	$ 1,341	$ 1,341	$ 1,341		
19. Subtract Cash Savings on Taxes					
(Line 15, Line 16, or Line 17)	$ 266	$ 241	$ 129	$	241
20. Monthly Payment Adjusted for Tax Savings	$ 1,075	$ 1,100	$ 1,212		
21. Subtract EQUITY Portion of Monthly Payment					
(Equity or Principal = Line 5 Minus Interest x Line 11)	$ 227	$ 227	$ 227	$	227
22. Actual Monthly Payment	$ 848	$ 873	$ 985	$	1,668
				What You Are	What You Are
				Paying to Own	Paying to Rent

(G) DIFFERENT MONTHLY PAYMENTS BASED ON AMORTIZATION

Comparison of Payments and Amortization

	Payment Option 1: 30 Yr	Payment Option 2: 25 Yr	Difference Option 1	Payment Option 3: 20 Yr	Difference Option 1
Monthly Principal & Interest:	$ 1 014	$ 1 104	$ 90	$ 1 246	$ 232
x Term of Loan in Months	360	300		240	
"= Total Principal & Interest	$ 365 040	$ 331 200		$ 299 040	
- Beginning Mortgage Balance	$ 188 800	$ 188 800		$ 188 800	
"= Interest Paid	$ 176 240	$ 142 400	$ 33 840	$ 110 240	$ 66 000

RENT-VS-BUY WORKSHEET
OWNER-OCCUPANT Showing Wealth Creators

FOR: _____   (1) Time DATE: _____

(A) PROPERTY DESCRIPTION		BUY	RENT

I. Description:	_____	(2) Not Paying Rent
II. Location:	_____	
III. Land Tenure:	_____	
IV. Down Payment:	_____	
V. Financing Terms:	_____	
VI. Tax Assumptions:	_____	

(B) FINANCING TERMS

1. Sales Price of Home	_____	(3) Appreciation
2. Cash Required for Down Payment	_____	(4) Leverage
3. Mortgage	_____	(5) Savings Account Called "Mortgage"
4. Other	_____	

(C) MONTHLY PAYMENT

5. Principal and Interest (P & I)	(6) Constant Monthly Payment	_____
(Line 5 - Line 11 = Principal)		
6. Deposit for Property Taxes (Approximate)		_____
7. Mortgage Insurance - Lender		_____
8. Maintenance Payments (AOUA)		_____
9. Other: _____		_____
10. Total Monthly Payments		_____

(D) ACTUAL MONTHLY TAX DEDUCTIBLE EXPENSES

Homeowner's Tax Deductible Expenses

11. First Month's Interest	_____	
(Line 3 x Interest Rate ÷ 12 = Interest Per Month)		
12. Monthly Tax Deposit	_____	(7) Tax Savings
13. Mortgage Insurance	_____	
14. Total Deductions	_____	

(E) CASH SAVINGS PER MONTH ON TAXES

(TAX BRACKET % x TOTAL DEDUCTIONS AS SHOWN ON LINE 12)

15. 31% Tax Bracket ($____ x 31%) Line 14 x 31%	=	_____
16. 28% Tax Bracket ($____ x 28%) Line 14 x 28%	=	_____
17. 15% Tax Bracket ($___ x 15%) Line 14 x 15%	=	_____

(F) DETERMINING ACTUAL MONTHLY COST OF BUYING
(WHEN ADJUSTED FOR TAX & EQUITY PAID)

	31%	28%	15%		
18. Total Monthly Payment (Line 10)	_____	_____	_____		
19. Subtract Cash Savings on Taxes	_____	_____	_____		
(Line 15, Line 16, or Line 17)					
20. Monthly Payment Adjusted for Tax Savings	_____	_____	_____		
21. Subtract EQUITY Portion of Monthly Payment					
(Equity or Principal = Line 5 Minus Interest x Line 11)	_____	_____	_____	(8) Principal	
22. Actual Monthly Payment	_____	_____	_____		
				What You Are	What You Are
				Paying to Own	Paying to Rent

(G) DIFFERENT MONTHLY PAYMENTS BASED ON AMORTIZATION

Comparison of Payments and Amortization   (9) Prepayment

	Payment Option 1: 30 Yr	Payment Option 2: 25 Yr	Difference Option 1	Payment Option 3: 20 Yr	Difference Option 1
x Term of Loan in Months					
"= Total Principal & Interest					
- Beginning Mortgage Balance					
"= Interest Paid					

RENT-VS-BUY WORKSHEET
INVESTOR (Showing Wealth Creators)

FOR: _____ (1) Time **DATE:** _____

	BUY
(A) PROPERTY DESCRIPTION	

I. Description: _____ (2) Receiving Rent (Refer to "D." below)
II. Location: _____
III. Land Tenure: Fee Simple
IV. Down Payment: ____%
V. Financing Terms: 1st Mortgage: ___-Year Mortgage / __% Interest
VI. Tax Assumptions: Owner-Occupant Using Itemized Deductions

(B) FINANCING TERMS

1. Sales Price of Home _____ (3) Appreciation
2. Cash Required for Down Payment _____ (4) Leverage
3. Mortgage _____ (5) Savings Account
4. Other _____

(C) MONTHLY PAYMENT

5. Principal and Interest (P & I) (6) Constant Monthly Payment _____
   (Line 5 - Line 11 = Principal)
6. Deposit for Property Taxes (Approximate) _____
7. Mortgage Insurance - Lender _____
8. Maintenance Payments (AOUA) _____
9. Other: _____ _____
10. Total Monthly Payments _____

(D) INCOME EXPENSE STATEMENT

I. Rent Income _____ (10) Income
II. Expenses (11) Expense
   1. Advertising _____
   2. Cleaning _____
   3. Insurance _____
   4. Legal Fees _____
   5. Maintenance _____
   6. Tax Prep Fee _____
   7. Management Fee _____
   8. Mortgage Interest _____
   9. Repairs _____
   10. Supplies _____
   11. Taxes _____
   12. Utilities _____
   13. Pest Control _____
   14. Painting _____
   15. Plumbing _____
   16. AOUO Fees _____
   17. Total £ Monthly £ Yearly Expenses _____
   18. Depreciation (12) Depreciation
   19. Total Expenses _____
                                    Total _____

Depreciation: Sales Price - Land Value = Depreciable Improvements	We Assume a 33 Year Life (Could be longer or shorter)

(E) CASH SAVINGS PER MONTH ON TAXES
(TAX BRACKET % x TOTAL DEDUCTIONS AS SHOWN ON LINE 12) (7) Tax Deduction Including Depreciation

15. 31% Tax Bracket ($_____ x 31%) Line 19 x 31% = _____
16. 28% Tax Bracket ($_____ x 28%) Line 19 x 28% = _____
17. 15% Tax Bracket ($_____ x 15%) Line 19 x 15% = _____

(F) DETERMINING ACTUAL MONTHLY COST OF BUYING
(WHEN ADJUSTED FOR TAX & EQUITY PAID)

	31%	28%	15%		
18. Total Monthly Payment (Line 10)					
19. Subtract Cash Savings on Taxes (Line 15, Line 16, or Line 17)					
20. Monthly Payment Adjusted for Tax Savings					
21. Subtract EQUITY Portion of Monthly Payment (Equity or Principal = Line 5 Minus Interest x Line 11)				(8) Principal	
22. Actual Monthly Payment					
				What You Are Paying to Own	What You Are Paying to Rent

(G) DIFFERENT MONTHLY PAYMENTS BASED ON AMORTIZATION

Comparison of Payments and Amortization (9) Prepayment

	Payment Option 1: 30 Yr	Payment Option 2: 25 Yr	Difference Option 1	Payment Option 3: 20 Yr	Difference Option 1
Monthly Principal & Interest:					
x Term of Loan in Months					
"= Total Principal & Interest					
- Beginning Mortgage Balance					
"= Interest Paid					

RENT-VS-BUY WORKSHEET
INVESTOR

FOR: _____   DATE: _____

(A)	PROPERTY DESCRIPTION		BUY	RENT

I. Description:	2-Bedroom /1-Bath	$ 1,200
II. Location:	Plantation Town Apartments	
III. Land Tenure:	Fee Simple	
IV. Down Payment:	20%	
V. Financing Terms:	1st Mortgage: 30-Year Mortgage / 5% Interest	
VI. Tax Assumptions:	Owner-Occupant Using Itemized Deductions	

(B) FINANCING TERMS

1.	Sales Price of Home	$ 236,000
2.	Cash Required for Down Payment	$ 47,200
3.	Mortgage	$ 188,800
4.	Other	$ -

(C) MONTHLY PAYMENT

5.	Principal and Interest (P & I)	$ 1,014.00
	(Line 5 - Line 11 = Principal)	
6.	Deposit for Property Taxes (Approximate)	$ 72.00
7.	Mortgage Insurance - Lender	
8.	Maintenance Payments (AOUA)	$ 255.00
9.	Other: _____	$ -
10.	Total Monthly Payments	$ 1,341.00

(D) INCOME EXPENSE STATEMENT

I. Rent Income	$ 1,200.00	
II. Expenses		
Advertising		
Cleaning		
Insurance	20.00	
Legal Fees		
Maintenance		
Tax Prep Fee		
Management Fee	120.00	(Prin. & Int.) (Int.) (Prin.
Mortgage Interest	787.00	Line 11: $1,014 - $787 = $227
Repairs		
Supplies		
Taxes	72.00	
Utilities		
Pest Control		
Painting		
Plumbing		
AOUO Fees	225.00	

Total £ Monthly £ Yearly Expenses	$ <1,152.00>
Depreciation	$ < 295.00>
Total	$ 1,447.00

Depreciation:	Sales Price - Land Value = Depreciable Improvements	We Assume a 33 Year Life
	$236,000 - $100,000 = $136,000	$136,000 , 33 Years = $3,540 Per Year , 12 = $295 Per Month

(E) CASH SAVINGS PER MONTH ON TAXES
(TAX BRACKET % x TOTAL DEDUCTIONS AS SHOWN ON LINE 12)

15.	31% Tax Bracket ($1,447 x 31%) Line 14 x 31%	=	$	448.57
16.	28% Tax Bracket ($1,447 x 28%) Line 14 x 28%	=	$	405.16
17.	15% Tax Bracket ($1,447 x 15%) Line 14 x 15%	=	$	217.05

(F) DETERMINING ACTUAL MONTHLY COST OF BUYING
(WHEN ADJUSTED FOR TAX & EQUITY PAID)

		31%	28%	15%		
18.	Total Monthly Payment (Line 10)	$ 1,341	$ 1,341	$ 1,341		
19.	Subtract Cash Savings on Taxes					
	(Line 15, Line 16, or Line 17)	$ 448	$ 405	$ 217		$ 241
20.	Monthly Payment Adjusted for Tax Savings	$ 893	$ 936	$ 1,124		
21.	Subtract EQUITY Portion of Monthly Payment					
	(Equity or Principal = Line 5 Minus Interest x Line 11)	$ 227	$ 227	$ 227		$ 227
22.	Actual Monthly Payment	$ 666	$ 709	$ 897	$ 848 to $ 985	$ 1,668
					What You Are Paying to Own	What You Are Paying to Rent

(G) DIFFERENT MONTHLY PAYMENTS BASED ON AMORTIZATION
Comparison of Payments and Amortization

	Payment Option 1: 30 Yr	Payment Option 2: 25 Yr	Difference Option 1	Payment Option 3: 20 Yr	Difference Option 1
Monthly Principal & Interest:					
x Term of Loan in Months					
*= Total Principal & Interest					
- Beginning Mortgage Balance					
*= Interest Paid					

Year 1 Month	Monthly P&I	Interest	Principal	Ending Balance	Interest to Principal	Cumulative	Interest to Principal Earned over Remainder of Loan
Loan				$188,800.00			
1	$1,013.52	$786.67	$226.85	$188,573.15			
2	$1,013.52	$785.72	$227.80	$188,345.35	$0.95	$0.95	$341.05
3	$1,013.52	$784.77	$228.75	$188,116.60	$0.95	$1.90	$340.10
4	$1,013.52	$783.82	$229.70	$187,886.90	$0.95	$2.85	$339.15
5	$1,013.52	$782.86	$230.66	$187,656.25	$0.96	$3.81	$341.76
6	$1,013.52	$781.90	$231.62	$187,424.63	$0.96	$4.77	$340.80
7	$1,013.52	$780.94	$232.58	$187,192.04	$0.96	$5.73	$339.84
8	$1,013.52	$779.97	$233.55	$186,958.49	$0.97	$6.70	$342.41
9	$1,013.52	$778.99	$234.53	$186,723.97	$0.98	$7.68	$344.96
10	$1,013.52	$778.02	$235.50	$186,488.46	$0.97	$8.65	$340.47
11	$1,013.52	$777.04	$236.48	$186,251.98	$0.98	$9.63	$343.00
12	$1,013.52	$776.05	$237.47	$186,014.51	$0.99	$10.62	$345.51

Year 15 Month	Monthly P&I	Interest	Principal	Ending Balance	Interest to Principal	Cumulative	Interest to Principal Earned over Remainder of Loan
180	$1,013.52	$536.01	$477.51	$128,164.82	$1.98	$250.66	$358.38
181	$1,013.52	$534.02	$479.50	$127,685.32	$1.99	$252.65	$358.20
182	$1,013.52	$532.02	$481.50	$127,203.82	$2.00	$254.65	$358.00
183	$1,013.52	$530.02	$483.50	$126,720.32	$2.00	$256.65	$356.00
184	$1,013.52	$528.00	$485.52	$126,234.80	$2.02	$258.67	$357.54
185	$1,013.52	$525.98	$487.54	$125,747.26	$2.02	$260.69	$355.52

186	$1,013.52	$523.95	$489.57	$125,257.69	$2.03	$262.72	$355.25
187	$1,013.52	$521.91	$491.61	$124,766.08	$2.04	$264.76	$354.96
188	$1,013.52	$519.86	$493.66	$124,272.42	$2.05	$266.81	$354.65
189	$1,013.52	$517.80	$495.72	$123,776.70	$2.06	$268.87	$354.32
190	$1,013.52	$515.74	$497.78	$123,278.92	$2.06	$270.93	$352.26
191	$1,013.52	$513.66	$499.86	$122,779.06	$2.08	$273.01	$353.60
192	$1,013.52	$511.58	$501.94	$122,277.12	$2.08	$275.09	$351.52

Year 30 Month	Monthly P&I	Interest	Principal	Ending Balance	Interest to Principal	Cumulative	Interest to Principal Earned over Remainder of Loan
348	$1,013.52	$53.33	$960.19	$11,839.14	$3.98	$733.34	$51.74
349	$1,013.52	$49.33	$964.19	$10,874.95	$4.00	$737.34	$48.00
350	$1,013.52	$45.31	$968.21	$9,906.75	$4.02	$741.36	$44.22
351	$1,013.52	$41.28	$972.24	$8,934.51	$4.03	$745.39	$40.30
352	$1,013.52	$37.23	$976.29	$7,958.21	$4.05	$749.44	$36.45
353	$1,013.52	$33.16	$980.36	$6,977.85	$4.07	$753.51	$32.56
354	$1,013.52	$29.07	$984.44	$5,993.41	$4.09	$757.60	$28.63
355	$1,013.52	$24.97	$988.55	$5,004.86	$4.10	$761.70	$24.60
356	$1,013.52	$20.85	$992.67	$4,012.20	$4.12	$765.82	$20.60
357	$1,013.52	$16.72	$996.80	$3,015.39	$4.13	$769.95	$16.52
358	$1,013.52	$12.56	$1,000.96	$2,014.44	$4.16	$774.11	$12.48
359	$1,013.52	$8.39	$1,005.13	$1,009.31	$4.17	$778.28	$8.34
360	$1,013.52	$4.21	$1,009.31	$0.00	$4.18	$782.46	$4.18
End of Year 30	$364,867.20	$176,066.98	$188,799.94			$107,134.22	$107,134.22

BONUS - REAL ESTATE JARGON

Appraisal: An assessment of a property's value by a licensed appraiser, often required by lenders to determine the loan amount.

Assessed Value: The value placed on a property by a local tax assessor for tax purposes.

Broker: A licensed professional who represents buyers or sellers in real estate transactions, often earning a commission.

Buyer's Agent: A real estate agent who represents the interests of the buyer in a transaction.

Closing: The final step in a real estate transaction where ownership is transferred from seller to buyer.

Closing Costs: Fees and expenses paid at the closing of a real estate transaction, including appraisal fees, title insurance, and transfer taxes.

Down Payment: An upfront payment made by the buyer at the time of purchase, usually a percentage of the property's purchase price.

Escrow: An arrangement in which a neutral third party holds funds or documents until the terms of a transaction are met.

Equity: The difference between the market value of a property and the amount owed on the mortgage.

FHA Loan: A type of mortgage insured by the Federal Housing Administration, often requiring a lower down payment.

Fixed-Rate Mortgage: A mortgage with an interest rate that remains constant throughout the term of the loan.

Good Faith Estimate (GFE): An estimate of the closing costs and other expenses associated with a mortgage loan provided by the lender.

Home Inspection: A thorough examination of a property's condition, usually conducted by a professional inspector before purchasing.

Homeowners Association (HOA): An organization in a community that enforces rules and regulations for property owners and often manages common areas.

Interest Rate: The cost of borrowing money, expressed as a percentage of the loan amount.

Insurance: Coverage to protect the property and its owner against loss, damage, or liability.

Joint Tenancy: A form of property ownership where two or more individuals hold equal shares and have the right of survivorship.

Lease: A rental agreement that outlines the terms and conditions under which a property is rented.

Lien: A legal claim against a property for unpaid debts, which can affect the sale of the property.

Mortgage: A loan used to purchase property, where the property itself serves as collateral.

Multiple Listing Service (MLS): A database of properties for sale used by real estate professionals to share information.

Negotiation: The process of discussing terms and conditions to reach an agreement in a real estate transaction.

Offer: A proposal made by a buyer to purchase a property at a specified price and terms.

Owner's Title Insurance: Insurance that protects the buyer against title issues not discovered before the purchase.

Pre-Approval: A lender's conditional commitment to providing a mortgage loan based on a buyer's financial status.

Property Tax: Taxes levied by local governments on real estate properties based on their assessed value.

Qualifying Ratio: A financial measure used by lenders to determine a borrower's ability to repay a mortgage, often including debt-to-income ratio.

Realtor: A real estate agent who is a member of the National Association of Realtors (NAR) and adheres to its code of ethics.

Rent: The amount paid by a tenant to a landlord for the use of a property.

Security Deposit: A sum of money paid by a tenant to cover potential damages or unpaid rent.

Title: The legal right to ownership of a property, often evidenced by a deed.

Terms of Sale: The conditions under which a property is sold, including price, financing, and contingencies.

Transfer Tax: A tax imposed on the transfer of property ownership, usually paid at the closing of the sale.

Underwriting: The process by which a lender evaluates the risk of offering a mortgage loan, including verifying financial information and property value.

Vacancy Rate: The percentage of unoccupied rental properties in a given area or property.

Warranty Deed: A legal document that provides a guarantee of clear title to the property being transferred.

Zoning: Local regulations that dictate how property in certain areas can be used, such as residential, commercial, or industrial.

ABOUT THE AUTHOR

Peter Savio

Born in Hilo and raised in Hawaii, he had real estate in his blood from an early age. His mother and father worked in the real estate and insurance business. His mother, Mary Savio, established Tropic Shores Realty in the 1950s, a well-known and reputable brokerage of its time. Buying his first home at 15 years old after saving money from his paper boy route, the real estate "bug" bit him early.

After serving in Vietnam and completing schooling at UH with an emphasis in real estate, he, *fast forwarding*, founded the Savio Group and became the largest condominium converter and lease-to-fee converter in the State of Hawaii. In the early 2000s, he filed for three bankruptcies and had to nearly sell everything, but bounced back and became known as "The Comeback Kid."

Peter Savio continues to conduct and develop projects he has become prolific for, lease-to-fees, and condo conversions, alongside exploring other opportunities—but most of all, he champions home ownership as a tried and true way to generational wealth. Lease or *legacy*.

In closing, he hopes to continue to share what he has learned through his long form, which is a curation of his decades of experience.

If you found this book helpful, be sure to check out his other titles such as ***Hawaii's Housing Solution "Move to the Mainland": 60 Years of Failure, IT MUST END***. Your read and support make a difference.

MAHALO!